How to Understand Business Finance

THE SUNDAY TIMES

How to Understand Business Finance

Robert Cinnamon, Brian Helweg-Larsen
and Paul Cinnamon
Second Edition

KoganPage

LONDON PHILADELPHIA NEW DELHI

Publisher's note

Every possible effort has been made to ensure that the information contained in this book is accurate at the time of going to press, and the publishers and authors cannot accept responsibility for any errors or omissions, however caused. No responsibility for loss or damage occasioned to any person acting, or refraining from action, as a result of the material in this publication can be accepted by the editor, the publisher or any of the authors.

First published in Great Britain in 2002 by Kogan Page Limited entitled *If You're So Brilliant... How Come You Don't Understand Your Accountant?*
Reissued in 2005 entitled *How Come You Don't Understand Your Accountant?*
Reissued in 2006 entitled *How to Understand Business Finance*
Second edition 2010

120 Pentonville Road	525 South 4th Street, #241	4737/23 Ansari Road
London N1 9JN	Philadelphia PA 19147	Daryaganj
United Kingdom	USA	New Delhi 110002
www.koganpage.com		India

© Robert Cinnamon, Brian Helweg-Larsen and Paul Cinnamon, 2002, 2006, 2010

The right of Robert Cinnamon and Brian Helweg-Larsen to be identified as the authors of this work has been asserted by them in accordance with the Copyright, Designs and Patents Act 1988.

ISBN   978 0 7494 6020 4
E-ISBN 978 0 7494 6021 1

The views expressed in this book are those of the authors, and are not necessarily the same as those of Times Newspapers Ltd.

British Library Cataloguing-in-Publication Data

A CIP record for this book is available from the British Library.

Library of Congress Cataloging-in-Publication Data

Cinnamon, Robert.
  How to understand business finance / Bob Cinnamon, Brian Helweg-Larsen. -- 2nd ed.
    p. cm.
  ISBN 978-0-7494-6020-4
  1. Business enterprises--Finance. 2. Financial statements. I. Helweg-Larsen, Brian. II. Title.
  HG4026.C526 2010
  658.15--dc22
                          2009045602

Typeset by Saxon Graphics Ltd, Derby
Printed and bound in India by Replika Press Pvt Ltd

Contents

Acknowledgements

Writing a book is a daunting task. I must firstly thank Professor Malcolm McDonald who told us that as a training consultant I should write books. Next, my colleague Peter Cheverton has provided an exemplary role model and inspired me to write a book on something I know a little about – finance for non-financial managers.

As an engineer by background I attended countless finance programmes, but it was not until I came across a hands-on business simulation that I really got to grips with the subject. The simulation was so effective that not only was I converted, but its models are now the basis of all my explanations on financial matters. A big thank you must therefore go to Nigel Downing and Brian Helweg-Larsen of ProfitAbility® Business Simulations for providing such an excellent mechanism for conveying in simple terms the sometimes difficult concepts of finance.

Lastly I thank my publisher Kogan Page for having the faith in me to produce a worthwhile book.

Robert Cinnamon
bob@cinnamon-ltd.com

I would like to thank Gordon Cousins for encouraging me to study, and then teach finance, and for working with me on the original ProfitAbility® design; Nigel Downing, for many years of friendship, working with me on Enterprise ProfitAbility® and building the business we run today; and my wife Sarah for her endless patience and total support.

Brian Helweg-Larsen
brian@profitability.com

Introduction

Many parts of this book build on the business game Enterprise ProfitAbility®, developed by ProfitAbility® Business Simulations. You will see a pictorial representation of the finances of a business in Chapter 2 and it will be referred to throughout the book. In other sections, examples will be given of six companies (Ace, Best, Cool, Demon, Excel and First) competing with one another in this business simulation and so again you can refer to the picture of the business in Chapter 2 if you find this helpful.

Readers who have a basic understanding of finance can dip in and out of the book at will. Others may find it helpful to read Chapter 2 first before moving on to more complex topics.

Inevitably, different elements of finance overlap. So, if you do not understand a concept mentioned in one part of the book, check to see if it is explained more fully elsewhere.

1

So why do you want to know more about finance?

Ask a group of business people why they need to know about finance and accounting, or more to the point, why they *want* to know about it, and the answers can be rather revealing. Most people say, 'I just want to know what they (the accountants) are talking about.'

This covers a variety of confusions from the abundant use of jargon (do you know your EBIT from your PBIT?), to the incomprehension over apparently arbitrary conventions (and yes, some *are* just arbitrary conventions...). The more vigorous the complaint, the more such comments betray a deeper problem. Typically, it is a face-saving way of saying that they don't really understand the principles of financial and management accounting. That includes reading a balance sheet – can you? And knowing how it differs from a profit and loss account – do you?

A variation and sophistication on this first response is, 'I'd like to be able to understand why what happens to me, happens to me.'

I have heard a marketing director say, 'The finance folk are a team along the corridor who reject my proposals.'

I have heard a production manager ask, 'Why is it that the CFO always wins when we are discussing budgets?'

The general cry of, 'It isn't fair...', when business people are confronted by their accountants, rises to a deafening climax when times are tough and cutbacks are required.

After these initial, and often rather bitter, responses, the more thoughtful will start to say that what they really want is the confidence to challenge their accountant's assertions.

The marketing director wants to know why she is always told that she spends her budget too quickly, and, more importantly, does she really?

The sales director wants to know why he is told to press customers to stick to their payment terms, or even to offer discounts for early payment, when what the customer really wants is extended credit, and in any case that big sales opportunity is just getting warm.

The operations director is told that he is sitting on too much stock, yet the salespeople always explode when they run out of something. What he wants to know is, what's the problem, and what's too much?

The buyer is pressed to ask suppliers for improved terms but what she would much prefer is for those suppliers to do her some *real* favours on developing new products. Who's right, the buyer or the accountants, and how could they discuss the pros and the cons of each approach?

Once you are able to discuss such questions, not only do the scales fall from the eyes but you are ready to move on to the next level of sophistication – actively managing your own financials.

If you run your own business, you will (at least in the early days) often be asking this next question of yourself. Why is it that when cash flow is good, I don't worry about it, I don't even look at it, but when it's bad it becomes an emergency demanding instant attention? At the point of crisis it is pretty difficult to pull anything out of the hat, and so most minds must turn to cost cutting.

You know it's short term, you know it will come back to haunt you, so why don't you act to avoid such situations in the first place? One reason might be because you were making handsome profits at the time. I have stopped counting the number of businesses that make handsome paper profits, but still go bust. But for more on that, you must read on...

Learning

There is little doubt that we learn best through experience and, very often, from hard experience. If you want to learn about finance there is no better way than jumping in, feet first, committing yourself to some stuff, digging your hole, and then fighting to get out of it. I would guess that the ex-directors of Woolworths now understand the hard realities of costs and cash flow better than most.

Now, you won't thank me for that advice if you were to practise it in your own business, so we'll aim to do it here, in someone else's. People who read books are simply trying to speed things up, and maybe avoid some of the bear traps. This book aims to give you that guidance, but also to help you with the experience of jumping in feet first.

We will explain the concepts, demystify the conventions, and translate the jargon by walking you through the set-up and first year's trading of a real company. But don't expect it to be plain sailing.

A tale of two languages

They say that the Brits and the Americans are two peoples divided by a common language, yet after years of *M.A.S.H., Monty Python, Friends and Fawlty Towers*, we seem to understand each other pretty well. We all know about those words that mark us out – lifts and elevators, boots and trunks, nappies and diapers, vacations and holidays – and any confusion caused in communication is rarely serious, only adding to the diversity of life. Personally, I like being offered cookies and suspect Americans are just as keen on being proffered a pint.

It only starts to get worrying when policemen controlling the crowds of Christmas shoppers on London's Oxford Street shout through their loud-hailers 'Stay on the pavement', and a dozen American tourists jump into the road – to these tourists the pavement is the road, and the sidewalk the pavement.

But how about when the words move from items of general discussion to those very specific references to business and finance? How much upset can you cause by sending an e-mail to a US colleague asking him or her to send you details of his or her *stocks*? Well, as you've just asked for a breakdown of his or her *shareholdings*, you'll probably be thought pretty pushy for a start. And if a US colleague asks you to detail your *inventory*? I have seen Brits send back a commentary on their R&D department – surely he or she means where we invent things, how quaint. Your colleague wants, of course, to know about your *stocks*.

Has a Brit CEO ever written to a US subsidiary saying that it really must cut its *expenses*, and fast, only to find that it has sold the factory? *Expenses* means fixed costs, while we tend to think of it as the travelling and entertaining budget.

Budgets is another term with all sorts of scope. By budget, the Brit means a well-thought-out set of targets and limits, whereas the Americans think of a low-price car rental firm, until you tell them you mean their operational plan. Asking them to send work on their budget, or to cut their budget, could have some interesting repercussions.

When an American asks a Brit what kind of *drawings* they will be announcing this year, they don't want to know about the sponsorship of the local arts festival, they mean *dividends*.

And so it goes on – the jargon and the terminology is just waiting to catch you out, 'both sides of the pond'. And just to add a complication, for the uninitiated, what purports to be English is not what you would find in the *Websters* – that's dictionary to us Brits.

Profit, a simple enough word, can mean a dozen different things, from gross to net, operating to post-tax, and some people still think of money, while the accountants would throw their hands up in horror at such a suggestion.

And on both sides of the Atlantic, accountants often have a whole series of synonyms for each concept, which they often use indiscriminately in conversation, causing total confusion to the layman. Add to this the fact that a number of very simple, well-known words, such as 'fixed' and 'variable', are used by

accountants with very specific technical meanings that have
virtually no relationship to their everyday usage, and you have a
recipe for complete frustration.

And then there are the acronyms – RONA, EBITDA, REM, ROE
et al. (Yes, the third one *is* a US rock band and not a financial term,
but who'd have dared to ask?)

In discussing the details of financial management we will aim
to explain these terms as we encounter them, and make no
apologies for using them in full where you might prefer to see
plain English – one of the ways of demystifying all this stuff is to
understand the lingo 'as she is spoke'.

Table 1.1 shows a list of some of the common terms in these
two rather different languages.

Table 1.1 Common terms in English and US English

English	US English	Other
Accounts	Financial statements	Books
Budget	Business plan	Operational plan
Creditors	Payables	Accounts payable
Debtors	Receivables	Accounts receivable
Depreciation	Amortization	
Dividend	Drawings	
Equity	Owners' funds	
Factoring	Cash discounting	
Fixed costs	Expenses	Burden, overheads
Funds flow	Cash flow statement	
Gearing	Leverage	
Gross margin	Gross profit	Contribution
Indirect costs	Sales, general and administration (SG&A)	
Internal rate of return (IRR)	DCF yield	
Loans	Debt	
Net profit	Net income	
Profit	Earnings	
Profit and loss account	Income statement	
Reserves	Retained earnings	
Return on sales	Return on revenue	
Sales	Revenue	Income, top line, invoice value
Shares	Stock	
Stock	Inventory	
Variable cost	Fluctuating cost	Cost of goods sold (COGS)

The business cycle

Setting up a company

Businesses differ to such a huge degree that each one is truly unique, and yet they all go through one simple process in much the same way. We will call it the business cycle. They produce and deliver a product or service, they invoice the customer, they pay their bills, they get paid by their customers, and they do the books. We are going to set up an imaginary company to demonstrate this process. The business is represented visually in Figure 2.1.

Let's take a look at our business. First, we're going to rent an industrial unit. This can accommodate up to four production units and the rent will be the same whether we have one unit or four.

We'd like to have some cash in this business. In reality this would be held in a bank account (or in your back pocket if you were a market trader!) but we'll have a cash box on our premises to place this cash in. Do we want to have a lot or only a little money in this cash box? Already we see a potential argument brewing between departments, so let's come back to this question in a later chapter.

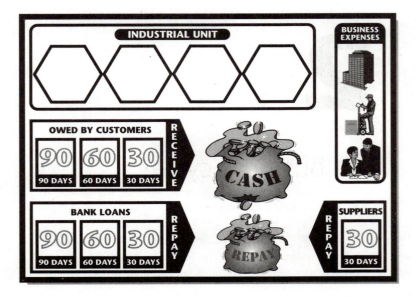

Figure 2.1 An imaginary business start-up

Next we'll have an area representing the money owed to us by customers. As you can see, we may have given our customers 30, 60 or 90 days to pay us and there is a box for each in our premises. When we deliver goods we invoice our customers and depending on the payment terms the money they pay should reach us in 30, 60 or 90 days. We can count that money but we can't have it yet! Month by month this money will move along, ever closer, until eventually it will come into the cash box – and only then can we spend it!

Underneath cash we have a 'repay' box. When anything hits this area we have to pay it from cash. If we don't have any cash we must find some or we are bankrupt. Never mind how much profit you are making, no cash means a bankrupt business.

On one side of this repay box we have the credit we can get from suppliers after we have been trading for some time and have established a track record. On the other side we have bank loans – again, once we have a track record and provided we meet the rules laid down by the banks we may be able to borrow from them.

Lastly, down the right-hand side we have various costs associated with running the business – rent, wages, administration overheads etc.

What would you need to start a new business? At the very minimum you would need:

- **An idea – a product or service. What is it you will be able to charge customers for (ie make a sale and issue an invoice)?**
- **Money – this is intentionally vague but you'll need some sort of funding.**
- **A plan – are you going to set up in your back room, rent an office, DIY or hire staff etc? The better your plan, the more likely your business is to survive and succeed.**

Let's say our idea is to go into business installing white burglar alarms. We're going to buy in the white burglar alarm system and we will charge people to install it in their homes.

Next we'll need some money. Let's represent this in grey casino chips – each chip being worth £1,000. We'll say that as owners of this company we'll put in £30,000 to start up the business. This is represented by 30 grey casino chips which we will place in cash, as shown in Figure 2.2.

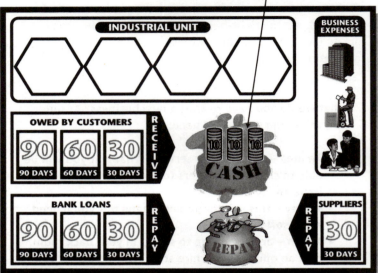

Figure 2.2 Cash for the business

The Moving Balance Sheet®

We're now going to invest this £30,000 in the business. We will want to keep track of where we spend this money; at least, our accountant will. We'll start a table recording what we have in the business and where the money came from. Obviously these two things should always balance (ie be the same), or else we could just give up working and 'cook the books' whenever we want a bit of cash to spend – while it lasts. This is shown in Table 2.1.

To install these white burglar alarms we are going to need some equipment – a van, ladders, tools etc, and we'll say this will cost us £5,000. So we'll buy this equipment and install it in our industrial unit. To pay for this we take £5,000 from cash and place it on the equipment. This is a visual representation of the value of that asset, as shown in Figure 2.3.

Table 2.1 Moving Balance Sheet® – Step 1

What we have:	Start business				
Cash	30				
Total	**30**				
Where it came from:					
Owners' funds	30				
Total	**30**				

The Moving Balance Sheet® is a registered trade mark of ProfitAbility Business Simulations

Let's look now at what we have in the business. We have £25,000 cash and the equipment valued at £5,000 making a total of £30,000. Generally accountants like to value things at what they cost. That's the *prudent* thing to do.

Prudence

You will know that the tax man is very fond of prudence, but you may not realise that all the accountants ever trained have had prudence drummed into them until it's part of their personalities. *Roget's Thesaurus* likens prudence to carefulness, sagacity, foresight, economy, caution etc. What it boils down to in practice is that accountants are trained to be cautious, risk-averse, and dubious about change.

'How do you know when you are talking to an extrovert accountant? They look at *your* shoes when speaking to you.' Of course, we all know the exception to this stereotype, but whatever an accountant's personality, prudence is not very exciting. An exceptional young accountant recently told us he was moving away from extreme prudence, but on a scale from 1–100, where 1 is extreme prudence, he reckoned he might now be on 5. Accountants are generally more inclined to hold you back than push you forward.

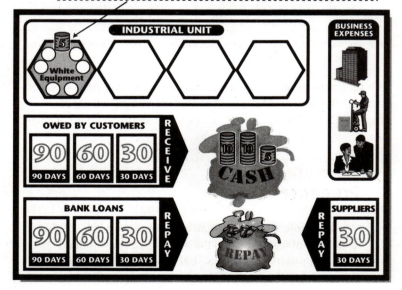

Figure 2.3 Value of equipment

Back to our record – where did the money come from? Well, *we* put the money in to start the business so we'll call it owners' funds and, as we put in £30,000, we balance, as shown in Table 2.2.

We're ready to move on to the next step – we need to recruit someone to work for us installing these alarms. Luckily there just happens to be a guy walking down the street who is fully trained and ready to start work for us. So we take him on and we're ready to go into business.

People – our greatest asset?

Let's look again now at what we have in the business. From the accountant's standpoint nothing has changed – and that's the value that accountants put on people: nothing! When the boss says that people are our greatest asset, you know that he or she is not an accountant.

There are a very few exceptions to this rule of not 'valuing' people – for instance, football clubs often pay huge sums of money for a player and so they put this 'asset' on the books and then of course expect it to make a return – they sweat the asset! But it's a risky business. That player has only got to break his leg and be unable to play again and that valuable asset is no longer worth a penny, whatever you say in the books.

Raw materials

To be able to install these alarms we're going to have to buy in the alarm components – the electronics, wiring, alarm bells and so forth. These raw materials are represented by white chips. If we look at our equipment we can see that there are six spaces for units of raw materials. That's because our operator, Fred, can only install six alarm systems in a month. There's no overtime and no night shift – he can only do six jobs a month.

Table 2.2 Moving Balance Sheet® – Step 2

What we have:	Start business	Buy equipment			
Cash	30	25			
Equipment		5			
Total	**30**	**30**			
Where it came from:					
Owners' funds	30	30			
Total	**30**	**30**			

The Moving Balance Sheet® is a registered trade mark of ProfitAbility Business Simulations

So here's a business problem for you: what are our options if we win a contract to install seven alarm systems this month? Well, we could deliver some this month and some next month. This is known as staged deliveries and can lead to all sorts of problems – batch to batch variation and disputes over how much has been delivered. We could subcontract someone else to install an alarm for us. Obviously we would need to pay that subcontractor and then invoice the customer ourselves for the work that has been done.

We could buy some more equipment – another van, ladders etc – and employ another person to install the alarms for us. Or we could buy a company that is already in this business: make an acquisition.

But let's come back to our little example and our record. We've agreed that we need to buy some raw materials. Each white alarm system costs £2,000.

As we have capacity to install six units a month, let's buy all six. We go to a supplier and the rep says, 'Never seen you before, so you'll have to pay cash.' So let's take delivery of the six units and we'll pay our supplier the £12,000 they cost from cash, as shown in Figure 2.4.

We now have £13,000 cash in the business. The equipment is worth £5,000 and we have some stock: £12,000 worth of raw materials – what we paid for them. This adds up to £30,000. Where's it come from? Well, it's the same £30,000 that we put in to start the company in the first place, as shown in Table 2.3.

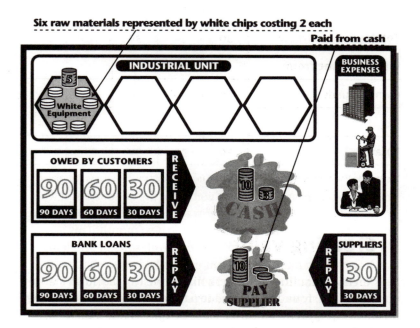

Figure 2.4 Buying raw materials

Table 2.3 Moving Balance Sheet® – Step 3

What we have:	Start business	Buy equipment	Buy equipment		
Cash	30	25	13		
Equipment		5	5		
Stock			12		
Total	**30**	**30**	**30**		
Where it came from:					
Owners' funds	30	30	30		
Total	**30**	**30**	**30**		

The Moving Balance Sheet® is a registered trade mark of ProfitAbility Business Simulations

Creating value

Let's review what this might look like in the real world. We've set up a company, found premises, developed a product and service, installed equipment, recruited staff, bought in raw materials, and now we are ready to sell those products and services. Have we added any value yet? Well, everything we have in the company is still only worth £30,000, which is the same as our original stake.

To 'create value' we need to sell something for more than it costs to supply. Let's say we find a customer who wants us to install five alarm systems and they are prepared to pay £20,000. We deliver the five white alarm units and the customer pays us our £20,000. The good news is we've made a sale – the bad news is that our customer is not going to pay us for 30 days. This £20,000 therefore goes on a box marked 'customer 30 days' to the left of the cash box as shown in Figure 2.5 and we will now have to wait until next month to receive these funds.

When is a sale a sale?

There are many potential answers to this, and here are some of them:

Salespeople say that it's when you get the order.

Accountants disagree. They don't go in for promises as a rule, and so will not put anything in the books based on orders. Worse, from the salesperson's point of view, the accountant will record all the costs of winning the order, with no recognition of the salespeople's hard work!

The legal department might say that it's when the signature is on the contract.

Accountants disagree again. Legally binding is not sufficient for them.

The common-sense answer is often: when we get paid. It is a long-standing cliché that the sale is not complete until the money is in the bank.

Accountants disagree yet again. They call a sale a sale at the point that an invoice is raised. When is a sale made in an accountant's eyes? It's when we can put it in the books and that is when we've issued an invoice!

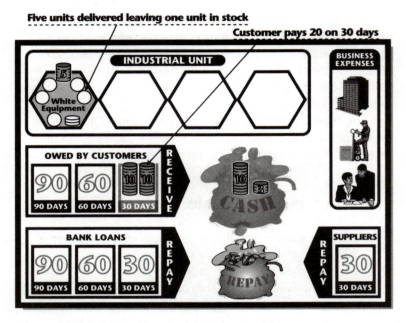

Figure 2.5 Delivery of goods and payment arrangements

If you're in a consultancy business you don't create value for your own business when you win a contract, not in the accountant's eyes. You don't even create value for your own business when you deliver the service. You create value when you invoice the customer and that could be some time later when you've prepared all your time sheets and you've calculated how much to invoice the client. At least, that's how the accountant sees it.

Cash and profit

Looking at what we have in the business now – we still have £13,000 cash, the equipment is still valued at £5,000, and we have something else we will call 'owed by customers': an outstanding invoice for £20,000. This all adds up to £40,000.

Where's it come from? Well, we know that £30,000 came from the owners. But can you see that the accountants can't now balance the books. So they invented something called profit, shown in Table 2.4. How much is it? Well, it must be £10,000 to balance the books!

This is an unusual way to demonstrate profit but we've done it this way to show that profit is simply a sum that the accountants do. You can't see it or touch it. In fact, there isn't a pile of £10,000 in sight. But what about cash? That you can see, touch and feel. You've only got to check in your cash box (the bank) to find out if you have any – we have £13,000, but profit was £10,000.

Table 2.4 Moving Balance Sheet® – Step 4

What we have:	Start business	Buy equipment	Buy stock	Sell 5 units for 20	
Cash	30	25	13	13	
Equipment		5	5	5	
Stock			12	2	
Owed by customers				20	
Total	**30**	**30**	**30**	**40**	
Where it came from:					
Owners' funds	30	30	30	30	
Profit				10	
Total	**30**	**30**	**30**	**40**	

The Moving Balance Sheet® is a registered trade mark of ProfitAbility Business Simulations

Cash and profit – not twin sisters

So cash and profit are not the same. This is perhaps one of the most crucial concepts of finance, and one of the most misunderstood. Profit is a sum, nothing more. Only cash is real.

Cash and profit – food and oxygen

Profit is like food. If you had nothing to eat for the rest of today, you would be hungry and might be cross, but you would be alive. Even after several days, perhaps weeks, you can keep going as long as you have air and water; and so it is for companies when they don't make a profit. But cash is like oxygen. No oxygen for several minutes, and you would be dead. No cash in a business, and within days it is also dead. Services are cut off, unpaid staff stop working, suppliers won't supply the materials you need, and the whole thing grinds to a halt. So, to keep the business healthy, you have to manage both: profit for the long term, and cash for the short term.

Lastly, what's going to happen in 30 days? Remember that customer who still owes us some money? Well, in the real world, after 30 days we may have to start chasing that customer to pay us but in our example we are paid on time. So cash goes up to £33,000, as shown in Figure 2.6, money owed by customers goes to zero and this still adds up to £40,000.

Of this, £30,000 came from owners' funds and £10,000 from profit, shown in Table 2.5.

We have seen that cash and profit are not the same, but do they change at the same time, and in the same way? Well, let's look at the

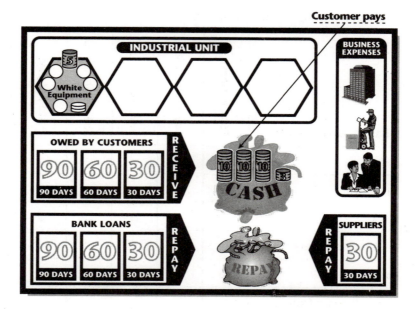

Figure 2.6 Receiving customers' payment

various activities that take place in any company. We buy equipment, raw materials, make a sale, collect money from customers etc on a regular basis. Between buying the raw materials and selling, did our cash change? No, cash was £13,000 before we sold the stock and £13,000 afterwards. What about profit? That went from zero to £10,000. So cash and profit are not the same although they are linked.

Now let's look at the effect of a customer paying an outstanding invoice. Cash leapt from £13,000 to £33,000 but profit remained at £10,000.

So, we've seen two examples of levers we can pull to affect our financial performance: making a sale (invoicing a customer) can generate a profit, while collecting money from a customer gives us cash but no additional profit.

What we have constructed here is a balance sheet – a statement of what we have in the company and how it is funded. Accountants call things we have 'assets' and things we owe 'liabilities'.

Table 2.5 Moving Balance Sheet® – Step 5

What we have (Assets):	Start business	Buy equipment	Buy stock	Sell 5 units for 20	Customer pays
Cash	30	25	13	13	33
Equipment		5	5	5	5
Stock			12	2	2
Owed by customers				20	0
Total	**30**	**30**	**30**	**40**	**40**
Where it came from (Liabilities):					
Owners' funds	30	30	30	30	30
Profit				10	10
Total	**30**	**30**	**30**	**40**	**40**

The Moving Balance Sheet® is a registered trade mark of ProfitAbility Business Simulations

Owners' funds – a liability?

So why are owners' funds a liability? Well, the owners might just want them back. Technically, the business owns nothing; it is run on behalf of the shareholders. In theory these shareholders could demand their funds back from the company. In practice, however, if a company is wound up they are the last to get paid. The first to be paid are the receivers or administrators called in if a business has ceased trading. Next is the taxman, then the banks, followed by suppliers, employees and, at the very end, if there is anything left, the owners.

We'll finish this section by considering the business cycle over time. Suppose we looked at our business over a month. Some of the activities we have considered happen at the beginning of the month – for instance, we might buy new equipment and recruit staff at the start of the month as it could take all month to commission the plant and train the staff. Depending on our payment terms our customers should pay us at certain times in the month.

And, of course, we expect to receive our salary on a set day of the month. How would you feel if your employer said, 'Bit short of cash, so I'm not paying your salary when it's due, you'll have to wait another week'?

So, in every business there is a specific business cycle with cash coming in and going out. Some of that is controllable by managers and other parts are non-controllable (eg tax and wages) – they have to be paid on a specific date.

Setting up and running the business – the opening month

Let's start with a clean sheet of paper and start this imaginary company again. Our opening month can be January. Once more we'll need some money to start up the business so we'll put £30,000 in cash into the business from the owners (see earlier, Figure 2.2).

Next we'll need to buy some equipment. As before we'll buy equipment to install white burglar alarms. We take £5,000 from cash to pay for the equipment and install it in our factory (see earlier, Figure 2.3). Now we need to recruit staff. In reality we don't just find someone walking down the street suitably qualified. We have to advertise or use an agency to recruit staff. Let's say this costs us £3,000. We take the £3,000 from cash and place it among our business expenses on the right-hand side of the board, as shown in Figure 2.7.

We are ready to start production so we'd better buy some raw materials. We go to our suppliers, and while they might be pleased to see us, we still have no credit rating, so they want us to pay cash for the alarm systems we buy. Buying five units this time will cost us £10,000, which we take from cash and place off the board – money going out of the company to pay for our raw materials, as shown in Figure 2.8.

Now we are all set to win some business. When we set up a new company, one of the first things we must do is to promote ourselves to get known in the market. We hope that this will

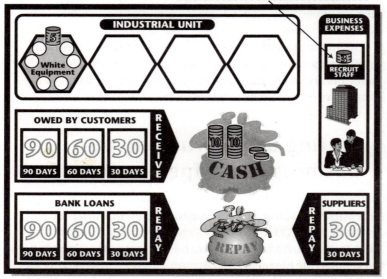

Figure 2.7 Recruitment cost

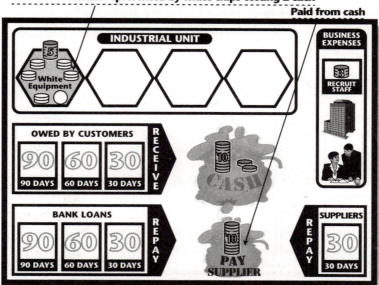

Figure 2.8 Cash payment for raw materials

generate some enquiries which will give us the opportunity to prepare some quotations. There is also a cost of preparing the quotations. In our example, we would have to go and survey the house where the alarm is to be fitted. We may have to make a sales call as well as preparing a written quotation. All this costs money. For this simulation, the cost of bidding for each order is going to cost us £1,000, and for this month we will prepare a quotation for just one order, as shown in Figure 2.9.

Generally, if well spent, the more we spend on promotion or business development the more enquiries we will get. But there is no guarantee that the more we spend on promotion the more orders we will get. The number of orders received depends on many factors, including our pricing, how we are perceived in the market place, the level of competition, our perceived quality etc.

So, we need to submit a tender document in order to win a contract. This would include the order number (in this case W1),

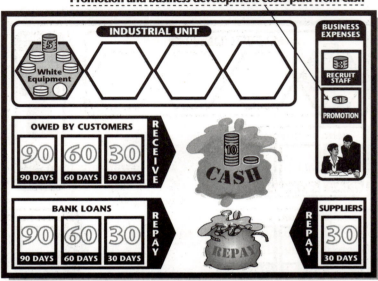

Figure 2.9 Bidding for orders

our company name, the credit terms (in this case 60 days), the number of units required (fortunately it is for five units – the same as this month's production) and a total price for the contract. In this case we will set a price of £30,000.

Let's say we submitted this tender and have won it. We pat ourselves on the back – the first rule in business is to win some contracts!

Before delivering the goods we must prepare our delivery record (as shown in Table 2.6). So, we are delivering order number W1, which is for five units, total price £30,000; the raw materials cost us £10,000 and we will make £20,000. Lastly we put the amount of money we will be paid (£30,000) in the 60 days' credit terms column. This is an example of what accountants call an audit trail – if the books don't balance they must be able to look back and track where the money should be coming in and going out. Most of this is now done electronically.

Table 2.6 January delivery record

Order number	How many sold?	Total price	What they cost?	How much you made?	Cash	Credit terms		
						30	60	90
W1	5	30	10	20			30	
Totals	5	30	10	20			30	

Now we can deliver and install the white alarm units from our premises to our customer.

We will receive £30,000 in payment for the installation of these alarms. Unfortunately, we're not being paid cash – the terms were 60 days, so the money will go on 'customers 60 days', as shown in Figure 2.10.

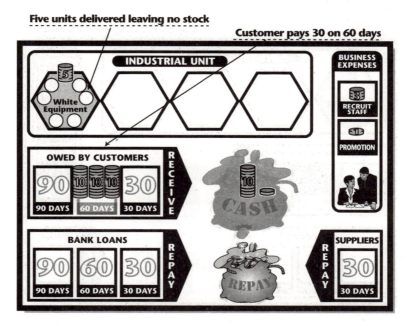

Figure 2.10 Receiving payment on 60 days

Having done all this, we'd better pay the bills. First, we'll need to pay our rent. We take this sum (£4,000) and place it in the expenses column on the right-hand side of the board in a box marked 'rent', as shown in Figure 2.11. Likewise, we place £4,000 in the box marked 'wages'. That will leave us with just £3,000 – not enough to recruit marketing, research, HR staff etc, not to mention accountants.

Profit and loss (P&L) account

We'll have to do the accounts ourselves. Starting with the profit and loss (P&L) account, shown in Table 2.7, we start at the top and work down.

The first thing we need to do is to calculate our sales. Taking our delivery record (Table 2.6) we add up all the orders by looking at the total price column. In our case there was only one order and

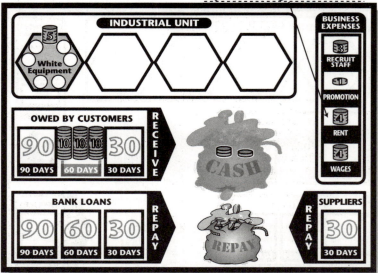

Figure 2.11 Paying the bills

Table 2.7 January profit and loss account (P&L)

	£000s	£000s
Sales	30	
Variable costs (costs of goods sold)	10	
Gross profit		20
Fixed costs:		
Recruit staff	3	
Promotion	1	
Rent	4	
Staff wages	4	
Total fixed costs		12
Operating profit (profit before interest and tax – PBIT)		8
Obligations:		
Tax	0	
Dividends	0	
Total obligations		0
Net profit (or net loss)		8

Note: One of the confusing things about real accounts is that there is no one set of conventions for the way they are laid out on a page. In this book we tend to use one column for details, and another to the right for important results such as totals and profit figures. Sometimes the figure on the right is the sum of those on the left (eg total obligations), sometimes it is one thing less another (eg gross profit, which is sales less variable costs). In a company's management accounts you will often see several figures with a box round them, in a single column; sometimes the figure above the box is the total of the things inside it, sometimes the total is below it, and sometimes the total is not shown.

this was for £30,000. Next we look at the cost of goods sold. This again comes from the delivery record in the 'what they cost?' column, in this case £10,000. So we have made £20,000.

Next comes our costs. These are found down the right-hand side of Figure 2.11 and are: recruit staff £3,000, promotion £1,000, rent £4,000, and staff wages £4,000, making a total of £12,000. So, we have made an operating profit – profit before interest and tax: PBIT (in the UK); or earnings before interest and tax: EBIT (in the US) – of £8,000.

We then have to consider what other obligations we must pay from this profit. First, there is the taxman. In most economies there is a tax holiday for new businesses to encourage new start-ups. So, we needn't pay any tax this month. Then we must consider whether we want to pay our owners anything out of the business so that they can make a return on the money they have invested in the business. This is known as a dividend and is normally paid from cash. As we don't have much cash our shareholders will have to be patient – we're paying no dividend this month!

This means our total obligations are zero and so we have a net profit for the month of January of £8,000.

There is one more calculation that is required now (as shown in Table 2.8). We start with retained earnings from last month (zero), add the net profit (or subtract a net loss), and this gives us retained earnings to date of £8,000.

The retained earnings figure goes across the page onto the bottom half of the balance sheet within shareholders' funds (shown in Table 2.9).

Table 2.8 January retained earnings calculation

	£000s
Retained earnings (or losses) from last month	0
Add net profit (or subtract net loss) from this month	+ 8
Retained earnings (or losses) to date (goes to balance sheet)	8

The balance sheet

As we have seen, a balance sheet is a snapshot at any point in time of what a company has and how it is funded (see Table 2.9).

Table 2.9 January balance sheet

	£000s	£000s
Assets (What we have)		
Current assets		
Cash	3	
Owed by customers (debtors/receivables)	30	
Stocks (inventories)	0	
Total current assets		<u>33</u>
Fixed assets:		
Equipment		5
TOTAL ASSETS		<u>38</u>
Capital employed: (where it came from)		
Owners' equity		
Share capital	30	
Retained earnings (or losses) to date	8	
Total equity		<u>38</u>
CAPITAL EMPLOYED		<u>38</u>

Note: The phrase 'balance sheet' is a breakthrough for so many people. Let's have on one sheet of paper a statement of the assets, wealth, and financial strength of the company. It is so simple to understand that the top half is what we have, and the bottom half is where it came from. These two halves have to be equal – they have to balance. So let's call it a balance sheet.

We start by adding up the assets of the business. There is £3,000 cash, £30,000 owed to us by customers, and no stock. This gives us total current assets of £33,000.

We also have one other asset: a white machine currently valued at £5,000. This gives us total assets of £38,000.

Where has this money come from? Well, £30,000 came from the initial stake the owners put in to start the company. Then there is a further £8,000 retained earning that we carried across from the P&L account (Table 2.8). This gives us capital employed of £38,000 as there is no other funding at this stage.

We've reached the first milestone in learning about accounts – we've balanced the books for January!

We're profitable, but are we going bust?

Having balanced the books, we must now clear the money off our expenses box on the right-hand side of our board – this is cash which has gone out of the business to pay the bills. We're now ready to move on to the next business cycle of February.

Month 2 business cycle

The first thing that happens in our February business cycle is that we update the money owed to us by customers. So everything moves along 30 days, as shown in Figure 2.12.

Once again, though, we don't feel any richer – the £30,000 owed to us from last month's delivery moves from 60 to 30 days but we must still wait another month for it to move to cash.

At the start of the month we must consider whether to expand and invest in more capacity. Before making this decision we must look at the market and decide whether there is sufficient demand.

To expand, all we need to do is buy more white equipment. This will cost us £5,000, which we must find from cash. But we have no cash. So, because we are constrained by a lack of cash we are unable to expand. Welcome to the real world!

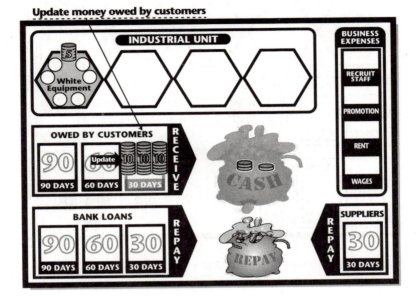

Figure 2.12   Updating records of money owed by customers

What about buying some more raw materials so that we can continue trading? Well, we now have a set of accounts and these have been audited and we've been given a credit rating. This means that we can get credit from our suppliers. So let's buy six units of white raw material for a cost of £12,000. The white stock goes into our production area onto the equipment. *Chequered casino chips represent money we owe.* So we must place 12 chequered chips on our 'suppliers 30 days' to indicate the £12,000 we owe our supplier for these raw materials and must pay next month, as shown in Figure 2.13.

As you can see, provided our customers pay us at the start of next month before we have to pay our suppliers, we will remain solvent (ie be able to pay our bills).

Buy six raw materials costing 2 each on credit

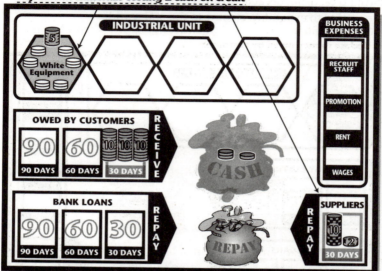

Figure 2.13 Money owed to suppliers

When is a purchase a purchase?

Not surprisingly, given the answer to the question 'When is a sale a sale?', accountants reckon a purchase to have been made at the date on the invoice. If buyers can persuade suppliers to delay sending them the invoices for a month there can be a month of buying nothing in the books.

Next we must consider promotion. Let's assume that there are six companies competing in our market, including ourselves. Table 2.10 shows a list of the contracts available for February. There are six different orders. Supposing we decide just to bid for order number W1. Only one company in our market can win this order, and what happens if it is not us?

Table 2.10 February orders

Order number	Quantity	Credit terms
W1	6	60 days
W2	12	90 days
W3	3	30 days
W4	18	60 days
W5	6	90 days
W6	12	60 days

So, if we agree it is high risk to just bid for one order we might consider the other extreme: bidding for all the orders. But this will cost us £6,000 and we couldn't deliver all the orders if we won them. As a compromise we'll spend just £2,000 on promotion and bid for two orders. We take the money from cash and place it on the promotion box within our expenses, as shown in Figure 2.14.

Now we must consider what price to quote for these orders. There will be a maximum price above which your customers can use a substitute product or service, resulting in their not even considering your offer. In this case the maximum price for a white alarm is £8,000. We will quote a total price of £37,000 on both our bids. We will bid for order numbers W1 and W5 and pay for and prepare the two tenders.

The market is tough and we win just one contract, order number W1. As we can deliver this contract from stock we will put it on our delivery record for delivery this month, shown as Table 2.11.

We have won order number W1, total price £37,000. The raw materials cost us £12,000, which means we have made £25,000. We deliver these goods and get paid £37,000 in grey casino chips. This goes on 'customers 60 days' according to the terms of the contract, as shown in Figure 2.15.

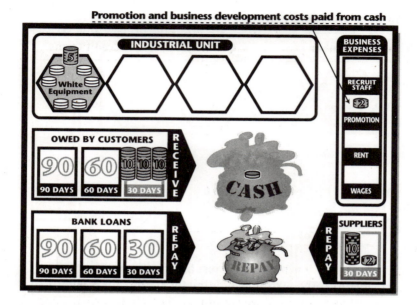

Figure 2.14 Promotion costs – bidding for two orders

Table 2.11 February delivery record

Order number	How many sold?	Total price	What they cost?	How much you made?	Cash	Credit terms 30	60	90
W1	6	37	12	25			37	
Totals	6	37	12	25			37	

Once again we've reached that point in the business cycle when it is time to pay our bills. The first one is rent of £4,000. But we only have £1,000 in cash. We're profitable but have run out of cash.

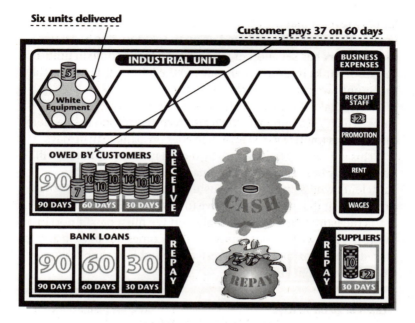

Figure 2.15 Payment for order number W1 on 60 days

Going to the bank

What are our options? One is to go to the bank for a loan. Banks are straightforward. They have a set of criteria you must meet to get a loan. Provided you meet their terms they will give you the loan. The trouble is that their terms are sometimes very onerous – they may insist on security (such as an owner's house) if it's a new company.

In our simulation the bank has a simple rule. It will match the amount of money that the owners have in the company. In other words, it is prepared to share the risk with the owners but not prepared to put more money in than the shareholders. If it did put in more, the bank would be taking more risk than the owners, and banks, like accountants, are prudent.

How do we find out how much the owners have invested in the company? Looking at the balance sheet from the end of

January reveals that the owners' equity is £38,000. So, the good news is that the banks will lend us up to £38,000. The bad news is that the bank has set another lending rule: loans come in units of £20,000. Banks interpret their rules to the letter – this means that this month we can only borrow £20,000.

So let's take this loan. We'll receive £20,000 in grey casino chips, which goes into cash. We'll also receive £20,000 in chequered casino chips (money we owe), which goes on 'bank loan 90 days'.

This will move along month by month until eventually it will hit the repay box. Then we can refinance the loan if there are sufficient owners' funds in the business to meet the bank's terms. Otherwise, at that time we will have to pay back the loan from cash.

Is the bank a charity? Definitely not! We must pay £1,000 in interest when we take out this loan. This comes out of cash and is placed on the box marked 'interest' to the right of 'suppliers 30 days', as shown in Figure 2.16.

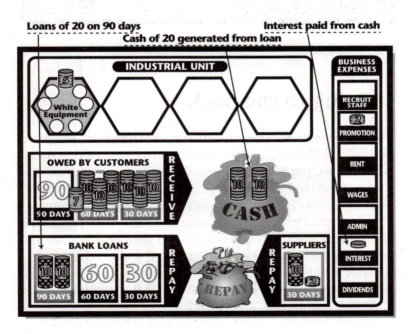

Figure 2.16 Paying bank interest

Now we can pay our bills. We must pay the following from cash onto the expenses boxes on the right hand side of the board. There is £4,000 for rent, £4,000 for wages and £4,000 for administration costs.

We ought to give the owners some sort of return on their investment too. We will pay a dividend of £4,000 paid into the 'dividends' box, as shown in Figure 2.17.

Doing the books

It's the end of the month and once again we can do our books. Starting with the P&L account in Table 2.12, we get our sales income from the delivery record (Table 2.11). This was £37,000. Costs of goods sold also comes from the delivery record and was £12,000. This means we made a gross profit of £25,000.

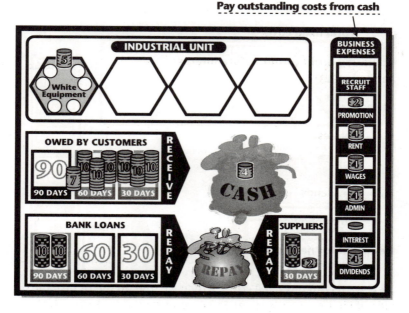

Figure 2.17 Paying outstanding costs

Table 2.12 February P&L

	£000s	£000s
Sales	37	
Variable costs (costs of goods sold)	12	
Gross profit		<u>25</u>
Fixed costs:		
Recruit staff	0	
Promotion	2	
Rent	4	
Staff wages	4	
Administration	4	
Total fixed costs		14
Operating profit (profit before interest and tax – PBIT)		<u>11</u>
Obligations:		
Interest	1	
Tax	0	
Dividends	4	
Total obligations		5
Net profit (or net loss)		<u>6</u>

Next we record our fixed costs, which we find on the right-hand side of Figure 2.17. We spent £2,000 on promotion, £4,000 on rent, £4,000 on staff wages, and £4,000 on administration costs.

This gives us total fixed costs of £14,000 and means we made an operating profit of £11,000.

Out of that profit we must now pay some additional obligations. We've got £1,000 interest and £4,000 dividend making total obligations of £5,000. So our net profit for February is £6,000.

Lastly we do the retained earnings calculation (see Table 2.13). We had retained earnings from last month of £8,000. We add the £6,000 from this month and this gives us £14,000 retained earnings to date. Again, this figure goes across the page to the bottom half of the balance sheet within owners' funds.

To do the balance sheet in Table 2.14 we freeze everything in the company and count it. We have £4,000 in cash. We add up all the money we have owed to us by customers (our debtors). This is £67,000. We have no stock, so current assets total £71,000.

Next we take away from this current assets figure the money we owe our suppliers, which is £12,000. This gives us net working capital of £59,000.

Lastly, we have white equipment currently valued at £5,000, giving us net assets of £64,000.

Where has this money come from? We have loans of £20,000, there was the original stake of £30,000 put in by the owners and there are retained earnings of £14,000 (from Table 2.13). This adds up to capital employed of £64,000.

And once more we've balanced a set of books.

Table 2.13 February retained earnings calculation

	£000s
Retained earnings (or losses) from last month	8
Add net profit (or subtract net loss) from this month	+ 6
Retained earnings (or losses) to date (goes to balance sheet)	14

Table 2.14 February balance sheet

	£000s	£000s
Assets (What we have)		
Current assets:		
Cash	4	
Owed by customers (debtors/receivables)	67	
Stocks (inventories)	0	
Total current assets (A)		**71**
Current liabilities:		
Credit from suppliers (creditors/payables) (B)		(12)
Net working capital (A–B)		**59**
Fixed assets:		
Equipment		5
NET ASSETS		**64**
Capital employed: (where it came from)		
Bank Loans		**20**
Owners' equity		
Share capital	30	
Retained earnings (or losses) to date	14	
Total equity		**44**
CAPITAL EMPLOYED		**64**

3

Where do all the business functions fit in?

While an understanding of the main financial accounts is of interest to business managers and financial analysts, if you work in one of the functions you could be asking yourself, 'Where do I fit into this?' The aim of this chapter is to show how each function is linked to the financial performance of the business, and how each can make its own contribution to financial health – we all have a part to play.

Sales

Sales teams obviously have an eye on the 'top line', ie sales generation. It is important to recognise the difference between sales volume (units sold) and sales revenue (monetary value). Salespeople frequently have no idea of the costs to provide the products and services they have sold and hence no idea of how profitable this piece of business will be. Sales bonuses based on profit rather than volume clearly motivate salespeople to understand this better!

Another area to watch out for is the discounts and commissions which may be offered. While these are variable 'costs' (ie if you don't make the sale you don't incur the cost), the impact they can have will be dependent on the dynamic of the business (see Chapter 11).

> Giving discounts for volume is a very slippery slope. Let's imagine a salesperson is with a customer, and that customer demands a price cut – not requests, you understand, but demands, 'Five per cent or there's no order'. She is, however, an understanding customer, and she knows that the salesperson will want something in return, so offers him some extra business. The question for the salesperson is: how much more volume is required if profit is not to go down?

The problem here is that most salespeople don't know the relationship between volume and profit, for one of two reasons: they don't know how to work it out; or even if they do know how, they don't have the necessary data to hand.

So what is it – 5 per cent more volume, 25 per cent, 50 per cent? The answer depends on what level of margin you were making in the first place. Table 3.1 illustrates this relationship between margin, discounts, and volume.

Example: if a business making a 25 per cent profit margin gives a volume discount of 7.5 per cent, a 43 per cent volume increase is required to make the same profit. (This calculation doesn't take account of any resulting economies of scale, or of the notion of marginal pricing and 'contribution to overheads', but even so, the figures are rather arresting.)

Table 3.1 is interesting, but remember that even if you have it to hand, if you don't know your margins in the first place it is not of much help.

Table 3.1 The percentage volume increase required to maintain profit, for discounts given

Discount given	Current % profit margin							
	10	**15**	**20**	**25**	**30**	**35**	**40**	**50**
2%	25	15	11	9	7	6	5	4
3%	43	25	18	14	11	9	8	6
4%	67	36	25	19	15	13	11	9
5%	100	50	33	25	20	17	14	11
7.5%	300	100	60	43	33	27	23	18
10%		200	100	67	50	40	33	25
15%			300	150	100	60	43	33
20%				400	300	133	100	66

Note: The figures in the main part of the table (shown in normal type) are the percentage increases in volume required for profits to stand still if a discount is given as shown in the left hand column, while the current profit margin is shown along the top row.

Know your margins

There are two main reasons why salespeople don't know their company's margins: their business systems are not able to measure margins with accuracy down to customer level; or the measurements are made, but the salespeople are not trusted with the information, for fear that they will tell the customer.

The dialogue between sales and finance has to improve such that accountants know why the need to measure margins at customer level is so important, and so that accountants can trust salespeople with this very sensitive information.

The tale of 'spreading jam'

A common problem is the way that businesses 'spread' their overhead costs across customers: that is, they spread them evenly, irrespective of the actual costs involved in dealing with different customers. They do the same when looking at product profitability, even at different business units – a laziness equally damaging to decision making. Take the following example of a company that talked itself out of business because of such 'jam spreading'.

The company has four customers, shown in Table 3.2: a profit in total, but the 'spreading' of overheads indicates a loss-making customer – customer D. The decision is taken to cease doing business with that customer. Unfortunately, overheads do not reduce immediately by the 60 that had been allocated to customer D, but they do go down by 30, and people give themselves a slap on the back for a smart decision.

Table 3.3 shows the new picture: the company is still in profit, but customer C is now a loss-making customer, and the troubled board meet to decide action. 'Concentrate on profitable customers', they say, and customer C is quietly dropped, but unfortunately, the overheads do not reduce in line. Table 3.4 shows the results of this move.

Perhaps you can guess what happened next.

The solution to this problem lies in some form of activity-based costing, where the costs of activities, people, overheads etc are allocated more precisely to individual customers. Businesses

Table 3.2 Consequences of 'spreading' overheads evenly – Customer D

	Customer A	Customer B	Customer C	Customer D	Company total
Gross profit	100	80	60	50	290
Overheads	60	60	60	60	240
Net profit	40	20	0	−10	50

Table 3.3 Consequences of 'spreading' overheads evenly – Customer C

	Customer A	Customer B	Customer C	Customer D	Company total
Gross profit	100	80	60	XXXX	240
Overheads	70	70	70	XXXX	210
Net profit	30	10	−10	XXXX	30

Table 3.4 Further consequences of 'spreading' overheads evenly

	Customer A	Customer B	Customer C	Customer D	Company total
Gross profit	100	80	XXXX	XXXX	180
Overheads	90	90	XXXX	XXXX	180
Net profit	10	−10	XXXX	XXXX	0

such as management consultancies, advertising agencies and legal practices will do this to some degree. What these companies sell is their experts' time, and so that time must be monitored and charged. The outcome is a business that knows where its profits come from, and so managers are better able to make decisions concerning key accounts.

Marketing

While sales is about present business, marketing is about the future. Here we find we are in uncharted territory. Marketers tend to think too much in terms of the P&L account, forgetting that developing and launching new products can have a major impact on production assets, stock, credit from suppliers, increased debtors etc.

In one case, a product manager enthused over a new product launch because he had calculated that it would make splendid margins, resulting in a very handsome P&L. Unfortunately, the long lead times for development, the huge demands on colleagues' time to get the project up and running and the massive building of stock in preparation for launch brought the company to its knees before it was able to invoice its first customer.

As well as considering these factors it may be appropriate to model possible marketing scenarios using tools such as discounted cash flow, net present value, and payback mentioned later in this book. In other words, to think of marketing activities as business projects with an initial investment and then subsequent income once the marketing has been implemented.

Manufacturing

Anyone who has been in production knows how accountants make people slaves to the budget. The biggest problem with budgets is that they are normally set at the end of the previous year, based on last year's costs. This sometimes bears no resemblance to what you actually end up manufacturing.

To overcome this problem, accountants invented 'standard costings'. The concept is based on devising what the ideal costs are for manufacturing each product you make. This includes an element of fixed costs as well as variable costs (see Chapter 11). Good in theory, but in practice we may manufacture it on different machinery, using different raw materials, in different batch sizes etc, never minding that we might have problems with the manufacturing process itself.

To compound this, some companies then introduce this standard costing into their management accounts. This means they value stock at the standard cost, which includes some fixed costs. When the product is sold, the value of this stock is taken across into the P&L account as normal, as part of the 'cost of goods sold'.

Fixed costs are also charged on the profit and loss account as they occur. This gives rise to a problem: we are in danger of double counting because there is also an element of fixed costs in the standard costings. Accountants remedy this by introducing 'recoveries'. This is the amount of fixed costs included in the standard costing of the goods sold in that accounting period.

All this confuses what is actually going on in the accounts to such an extent that you often don't know what's happening in the business! As you can guess, I am not a fan of standard costings except as a mechanism to ensure we monitor our manufacturing costs against some benchmark.

Clearly, manufacturing has a major impact on the accounts in terms of variable costs (raw materials, packaging, plant efficiencies etc) and fixed costs (direct expenses associated with production), and thus the profitability of the business.

Supply chain management

Supply chain managers have an impact on all stages of the production and sale of goods and services. Listed below are just a few examples:

- **raw materials costs, location and size of stocks and supplier payment terms;**
- **location of each phase of production, size and location of stocks of intermediate products, transfer pricing and local tax payments;**
- **choice of packaging and transportation;**
- **distribution channels, commissions, rebates etc;**
- **outsourcing, toll manufacture and subcontracting elements of manufacturing.**

All of these clearly have implications for variable and fixed costs, working capital and tax – in other words, the overall profitability of the business.

Human resources

Without the right people with appropriate skills and experience, our business cannot thrive. And yet we know that while we are told that people are our most valuable asset, they do not appear in the accounts except as a cost.

To make sure that we do not have additional unplanned costs for our staff, we need to have well-defined terms and conditions of employment, so that employees do not expect that the organisation will pay unplanned expenses. This can also be important when we second staff overseas, or have to terminate their employment.

Accountants will also view costs like training and development as optional expenses. These are often the first to be cut in difficult times. It is worth considering the impact that these activities have on the ability of your business to retain its staff. Recruitment and training is both costly and time-consuming, any savings must be compared with the costs and impact of recruiting, training and using new and inexperienced staff, which can be very great.

IT, maintenance and engineering

Nobody likes being lumped into 'support services' but IT, maintenance and engineering have similarities regarding their impact on finance. First, they are all seen as fixed costs to be managed.

All these activities are involved in purchasing new assets. It should not be forgotten that when you purchase fixed assets (plant and equipment) which have a useful life spanning more than one year, they should be put on the balance sheet as a capital item. This means that the total cost of these assets is removed from the

P&L account. Admittedly these assets are then depreciated, and this will impact on the profit (see Chapter 10). It is possible to suspend depreciation if an asset is mothballed, but your accountants will have a view on the *prudence* of such an action.

When undertaking projects whose effective life spans more than one year, you can think about capitalising the project costs and amortising them over the project's life (see Chapter 10). This has the effect of removing some of the costs from this year's accounts (increasing profits this year) and spreading them over future years. So, for instance, if you have a shutdown or system upgrade every three years you could spread the cost over this total period, rather than taking the hit on your profits in the year in which you undertake the project. Again talk to your accountants if this option is of interest to you.

We also need to carry spares to maintain our systems and equipment. The value of this stock is considered a part of working capital. In my experience, when you come to need the spare it is often in poor condition (assuming you can find it) or you have carried out a modification since the part was purchased so it does not fit. Consider getting the equipment supplier to hold the spares for you, tied in to a service-level agreement defining response times etc for delivery. While more expensive when you do need the part, this can eliminate some working capital and puts the onus on your supplier to maintain up-to-date spares, rather than yourself.

Often the systems and equipment we maintain enable our company to manage the business. This puts us at the heart of monitoring and delivering bottom line profit performance.

Research and development

The trouble is that the world never stands still. There are almost no products that can be sold for 10 or 20 years without being changed, or even replaced by newer technologies. The future of a company rests on its ability to develop products and services to keep up with or stay ahead of the competition.

Meeting customer needs for your products and services *in use* is another area where your development staff are involved. Also known as application development, this can be essential to keep and grow your customer base.

Being there first with new technologies (or applying technologies from other industries to yours) means you can charge a premium price, and if costs can be contained this can lead to better profits. Equally, R&D can lead to reduced production costs, which also improves profits.

Like the functions above, R&D can be treated like a project and financially evaluated before embarking on any expensive work. It too can be capitalised and amortised over the sales of a new product (see Chapter 10).

It is important to measure the effectiveness of your R&D in terms of the returns it makes for you, the percentage of sales generated from new product developments and the speed of getting new products to market.

Lastly, R&D can be invaluable in protecting the organisation against false complaints or claims (which if paid out would be included as additional fixed costs).

Finance

The finance department are often seen as the 'abominable no-men' policing what we can and cannot spend our money on. Without the accountants we really are trying to run our business blind. They have the power because they have the information.

So, get to know your accountants – they will share the information with you if you have a sound case for their doing so. They will listen to your concerns about fixed cost allocations etc if you have a reasoned argument, and are not just trying to push the costs onto someone else's budget. Let them do the analysis and then challenge the source of their data.

Using this book, you can understand the concepts, and that should give you the confidence to befriend your finance department! And you have to work together if you hope to improve your business performance.

Lastly, as you will see in the next chapters, accountants only record what has already happened – not always a sound basis for deciding what to do in the future.

4

Financial planning – the budgets

One of the problems with many of the reports that our accountants produce for us is that they are based on the past. The P&L statement cannot be completed until 'the books are closed' at the month end, and by the time this information is published it is stating what has already happened, in the last accounting period. It has often been said, unkindly but not always undeservedly, that accountants who run businesses are like motorists who drive with their eyes permanently fixed on the rear view mirror. Understanding the past is of huge value, but it rarely makes a good road map for the future.

Budgeting

Ever keen to oblige our complaints on this subject, accountants have overcome this problem by asking us to forecast or plan our finances, using a budgeting process – so we only have ourselves to blame. As anyone who has to manage a budget knows, this can be a highly academic process, not to say political, but the aim is to try to replicate what the next P&L account will actually look like.

A budget might include any of the following:

- sales income split into volume and selling price of each product, less variable cost of goods sold (COGS) including raw materials, packaging and distribution costs;
- budgeted gross profit, less direct and indirect fixed costs;
- budgeted operating profit, less interest, tax and dividends;
- budgeted net profit.

So, a budget (called a business plan in the United States) is an attempt to anticipate future sales, costs, and likely profits – or, in other words, it is a 'wish list'.

Cash flow forecast

We all know that cash is essential to put any plan into action, but it is incredible how many business people fail to consider the cash flow implications of their budget. This brings us to a second planning process known as *cash flow forecasting*.

There are many cash requirements not included in our budget above. For instance, what about the purchase of new assets or payment of outstanding loans? A cash flow forecast may therefore include the following:

- opening cash balance
  - add cash due from customers
  - less payments to suppliers
  - less cost of new equipment
  - less promotional costs;
- interim balance
  - add deliveries for cash (ie cash or credit card payments on delivery)
  - less direct and indirect fixed costs
  - less loan or interest payments
  - less tax paid out in cash (usually from the last accounting period)
  - less dividend payments to shareholders;
- closing cash balance.

There is no such thing as negative cash! If you run out of cash you are bankrupt. In the United States companies can 'file for Chapter 11', which means the government appoints administrators to try to keep the company going through their cash flow problems, thus maintaining people in employment. In the UK a receiver is appointed to try to sell what it can in the business to generate cash to pay outstanding bills. This is known as liquidating the assets.

The aim of the cash flow forecast is to anticipate problems before you run out of cash so that you can either modify your plans (and so also the budget) or consider additional funding to find the cash to make the plan work. There is no sin in having cash flow ups and downs – indeed, it would be a strange business that never experienced this roller-coaster ride – but it is a flow that can be managed, ahead of times.

Avoiding bankruptcy: how to generate cash

Supposing you have realised you are going to run out of cash. What can you do to generate cash?

Chasing payment

An obvious place to start is by chasing your customers for payment of outstanding invoices (your debtors). There is often no connection between your finance department (who may be having difficulty getting customers to pay) and your delivery department (who continue to provide goods and services to these bad payers), making the problem even worse.

The cause of having a large number of debtors can be a failure to negotiate and then police credit terms firmly with your customers. Most companies also set a credit limit on their customers to prevent the amount outstanding becoming too great.

Slowing down payment of bills

Slowing down the payment of your suppliers will not generate cash, but will stop it going out the door. In other words, most companies get their suppliers to fund their business to a greater or lesser degree. This is why the US convention is to have your creditors on the bottom half of the balance sheet (where the money came from).

Some caution needs to be exercised in applying this idea, as it is often regarded as the first sign of a company in trouble. When your customers blame a new administrative system for their late payment, you might wonder if it has cash flow problems, and what that might mean for their future, and yours. Good business practice suggests we should always try to negotiate extended credit terms, but not simply take them.

Selling assets

Clearly, we do not want to sell assets which we will need to run the business in the future. However, there are other assets which could be sold to generate cash. If there are redundant assets which are not being and have no likelihood of being used, we should consider selling them to release cash. Cash generated in this way sometimes comes from unusual sources. There was a businessman in the north of England who bought an old Army depot and sold the rails from an old railway system for scrap, gaining more than he paid for the site and turning himself into a millionaire.

You can even 'sell' your debtors (customers who owe you money) and turn money owed to you tomorrow into cash today. This is called factoring. You go to a factoring house (most banks can provide this facility) and offer to sell the invoices you have issued to customers which have yet to be paid. Depending on who the customer is, what the credit terms are and the level of risk involved, the factoring house will charge a commission based on the face value of the invoice and give you the cash today. A useful trick, you might think, but beware, like credit cards it looks cheap but costs you dear.

Supposing the factoring house charges you 5 per cent to give you cash for an invoice that is due to be paid next month. It seems quite reasonable, but if it costs you 5 per cent for one month's credit, what is the annual interest rate you are paying? Small businesses often get into the factoring spiral where each month they bring forward monies from 30 days. In the following month they have nothing coming in and so have to factor the next 30 days. In the end, because they factor invoices every month for 12 months, they end up paying an effective rate of 79.6 per cent – a very expensive way of funding your business.

Factoring has its place, but like paying your bills late it can make those in the outside world believe you are in trouble. Why not consider securitisation (see below) instead?

Going to the bank

As we have seen, banks are happy to lend you money as long as you meet their rules. Of course, when cash is tight, this is often precisely the time you *cannot* meet these terms.

Banks are also happy to lend you money when you can secure the loan against some assets. It is currently fashionable to negotiate extra loans using your debtors as security so that if you fail to repay the loan the bank will be able to seize your debtors. It's like factoring, but only when you really need to. Receiving additional loans in this way is known as securitisation of your debtors.

Going to the shareholders

Just how easy it is to go to the shareholders will depend on the size and make-up of your company. In a small family-run business it may be possible to go back to the owners and ask for more money (ie appeal to relatives). In a large company with shares quoted on the stock exchange, appealing to shareholders is much more difficult.

In a large company, selling more shares to your shareholders is known as a rights issue. Normally you need a good reason to ask shareholders to put more money into a business. Asking for a cash injection because of cash flow difficulties is not considered a good reason but rather a sign that the company is being run badly.

Get more business

While getting more business will not ease an immediate cash flow problem it should help in the coming months as the cash starts to flow in once more. It is essential, though, that this business is profitable. In other words, the sales income must eventually generate more cash than the costs going out or this will just become a greater drain on your cash. Of course, getting more business has a cost – there is the new sales effort, the promotional spend – and in the short term this will make your cash flow problems even worse. Spending your way out of cash flow problems can work, but is high risk – not what your accountant would call prudent.

5

Measuring business performance – financial ratios

Table 5.1 gives a summary of the financial performance of six different companies.

Which company is the best? It is difficult to say, and that is why accountants have invented financial ratios – to allow us to compare one company's performance with that of another. When doing this we ought to be sure that we are comparing like with

Table 5.1 Financial performance

	Company					
	Ace	Best	Cool	Demon	Excel	First
Annual sales (revenues)	100	120	150	160	180	200
Gross margin (gross profit)	80	80	75	90	100	140
Profit (earnings)	10	12	18	18	18	18

like, those famous apples and pears – a pharmaceuticals business compared to a chemical company may well not be considered a fair or useful comparison. For one thing, the level of risk in each is very different, leading to different expectations of what returns these organisations should make.

The corollary of this statement is that a financial ratio in isolation is meaningless unless we can compare it to another figure, a benchmark of some kind. We tend to do this intuitively when calculating these numbers by relating it to a known target or level of business performance.

Our competitors, at least the good ones, might make good benchmarks, only they rarely publish accounts broken down to the level required for us to make these comparisons. Even if they do, the ratios used by one company might well be defined rather differently in its accounts from the way you would understand them. We are back with our apples and pears again. In practice, companies tend to evaluate their performance against last year, against budget, or against corporate targets sent down from on high. None of these are very satisfactory benchmarks, since one is history and two are inventions!

Interpreting ratios can also be misleading. You need to know some background to an organisation to be able to explain its ratios. Analysing percentage gross margin (explained below) demonstrates this well.

All these ratios are based on a period of trading and a snapshot of a company's assets. Quoting these ratios to several decimal places can lead to some meaningless comparisons – if the ratios are close then so are the two performances. Try to avoid spurious accuracy or you could turn into an accountant, and remember we are only trying to understand them...

To overcome the short-term nature of ratios, some companies will look at an average figure over a period of time (eg Shell use a measure of ROACE – return on average capital employed).

Another issue is whether the accounts are quoting the same period of sales. Accountants will often 'annualise' the sales by multiplying the figure to represent 12 months' activity (eg multiplying a quarterly figure by four), but this can be misleading if a business is seasonal, or a major external event (eg global downturn or a major incident in the industry) has occurred.

Size

In terms of size, sales (or revenues) by value is most often used as a measure of who is biggest. Using this measure, First is clearly the largest company in Table 5.1. Other measures used might be sales by volume rather than value, profit, number of sites (eg supermarkets), employees (for service-based industries), product range, brand awareness, or even hits on the company's website.

It is also worth remembering that there is no point having the largest sales if these are not profitable. We need to make a trading profit, also known as profit before interest and tax (PBIT) or operating profit, as there are various obligations a company must meet from this profit. These are interest, tax and dividends.

Dividends are often considered to be a way of distributing the profits of a company back to its shareholders. This can be misleading. A dividend is usually a cash payment to the shareholders. In other words it comes from cash! It is because a dividend reduces the amount of net profit that is retained in a company that people talk about it coming from profits.

After paying interest, tax and dividends, whatever is left of the profit is left in the company to fund future activities. This is why it is often known as retained earnings and is carried across to the bottom half of the balance sheet.

P&L account (income statement) analysis

The basis of P&L account analysis is to consider each element compared to the sales or revenues value (also known as the top line). Sales shows the level of activity in this accounting period, and the costs that should be linked to that activity.

Gross margin (gross profit) percentage

Gross margin percentage is the gross margin divided by sales, expressed as a percentage. In the example on page 67, Ace has a gross margin percentage (GM%) of 80 per cent, Best 67 per cent, Cool 50 per cent, Demon 60 per cent, Excel 56 per cent and First 70 per cent. Using this measure, Ace is the best performer. GM% is a measure of how much profit you are making on each unit of sales after variable costs alone. Clearly, we would like this to be as high as possible. GM% is not volume dependent because units of sales are used to calculate both the top and bottom figures of the equation. Hence, you can sell one unit of business at very high margins and still make a loss!

Only two things influence GM%: the selling price and the variable costs. The sales team are often the butt of criticism for poor gross margins – with people saying, 'It's those prices they give our stuff away for...' We should remember that there are two parts to GM%, and we should take a long, hard look at the variable costs:

- **Variable selling expenses (VSE) – These include delivery costs, insurance, commissions, rebates and discounts, some of which are negotiated by sales staff, and some of which are part of the supply chain costs.**
- **Raw material costs – We tend to point the finger at our purchasing departments, which are responsible for raw**

material costs. However, raw material efficiencies or conversion rates, and levels of rework and waste, often have a large impact on GM%. The decision whether to make ourselves or buy in from others (toll manufacture, subcontracting, purchase for resale or PFR) can also affect GM%.

- **Product mix** – When selling a range of differently priced (and costed) products and services, a change in the split between higher margin and lower margin items can affect GM%. This is often hard to prove in a business selling many different products and services, and so is a favourite management excuse if GM% is below target.

Costs to sales (percentage)

Costs to sales is a popular measure used on many of the fixed costs in the P&L account. Depending on the type of business, different ratios will be used. For instance, a company selling consumer products may examine its advertising and promotional costs as a percentage of sales while a biotechnology company may look at research costs as a percentage of sales.

Profit before interest and tax (PBIT)

Profit before interest and tax is a common level of profit used for many ratios. In large companies, interest and tax are managed centrally, but in each business unit or division, this is the level of profit that managers control. Traditionally it has also been used because there are different levels of interest and tax in different countries and we can therefore compare more accurately across borders if we use PBIT. Today, many companies negotiate funding globally and arrange transfer pricing between countries to make the profits in tax-friendly locations, and so this convention is becoming less relevant.

Return on sales (ROS) (or profitability)

Return on sales is profit (or earnings) as a percentage of sales, and examines performance in relation to the bottom line (profit or earnings). In the example on page 63, Ace, Best and Excel have an ROS of 10 per cent, Cool 12 per cent, Demon 11 per cent and First 9 per cent. Hence, on this metric Cool is delivering the highest return of 12 pence in every pound of sales revenue.

If ROS falls from one period to the next, but GM% does not, this indicates either a loss of sales volume or an increase in fixed costs. A line-by-line analysis of each cost (or expense) as a percentage of sales can also indicate where management attention may be required.

When you look at financial ratios, it is important to ask three questions:

- **How does it compare (with last year, another division, or a competitor)?**
- **Why is it different?**
- **Is that good or bad?**

For example, if our GM% has fallen since last year, is that because we are discounting our prices, have raised our cost of manufacture or service in order to improve our image and move upmarket, or have entered a new market for mass sales of the product at lower prices, without changing our relationship and pricing to existing customers? And in each case, is that a good thing that we should continue or increase, or a bad thing that we should find ways to reverse?

Balance sheet analysis

In the example in Table 5.1 we can see that four of the companies are delivering the same overall level of profit (or earnings) and that when compared to levels of sales (or revenues) Cool is best. But what resources are tied up in generating these sales? This leads us to an analysis of the balance sheet.

Table 5.2 shows some of the elements of the top half of a balance sheet (the assets we have in a company).

Generally, there are two main elements – working capital and fixed assets.

Table 5.2 Company assets

	Company					
	Ace	**Best**	**Cool**	**Demon**	**Excel**	**First**
Working capital:						
Stock (inventories)	10	12	10	14	16	18
Debtors (receivables)	12	12	30	30	30	30
Creditors (payables)	(8)	(14)	(20)	(12)	(14)	(18)
Net working capital	14	10	20	32	32	30
Fixed assets	20	25	30	30	35	35
Net assets	34	35	50	62	67	65

Working capital

Working capital is generally made up of three elements: stock, debtors and creditors. This information can normally be found on any balance sheet (for instance in Table 2.14).

Stock (inventories)

As already pointed out, accountants value things at what they cost. There are four main types of stock or inventories:

- **Raw materials – When raw materials are sourced from different suppliers or at different costs, the accountant's task of correctly valuing this stock can be a nightmare!**
- **Work in progress (WIP) – Any goods, between leaving raw material stock and being passed as suitable for sale, are classed as WIP. In a multi-stage process this can become a considerable value, especially if WIP has to be moved between sites to complete production. Again, if the same items are produced at different sites at different costs, another headache awaits the stock keeper at month end.**
- **Finished goods – These are valued at what they have cost to make (or buy in for resale). The same problem exists in valuing this stock.**
- **Engineering spares – In a business with specialist equipment, considerable quantities of proprietary spares may have to be held to limit any machine downtime when breakdowns occur. There is always a trade-off to be made, and often a company will have a breakdown spares and maintenance contract with its equipment supplier, rather than holding these items in stock itself.**

Deciding the correct levels of stock is not simply a financial consideration, as stock is often equated with service levels or lead times. Also, simple comparisons to sales can be misleading, as unit for unit a different value is assigned at each stage in manufacture.

Debtors (receivables)

This is the total amount of money owed to us by customers. How do we know what is the right level? We can compare it to the level of sales, calculating days of sales outstanding (DSO or debtor days) using the following sum:

$$\frac{\text{Debtors}}{\text{Sales}} \times \text{numbers of days in accounting period in which sales generated}$$

Hence the DSO for Ace is 44 days, Best: 37 days, Cool: 73 days, Demon: 68 days, Excel: 61 days and First: 55 days. Immediately we see 37 days as the target to beat.

> **It is hard when examining the value of debtors on a balance sheet to decide what is a good DSO figure. Hence, accountants use the DSO ratio to enable us to make this judgement. DSO represents the average amount of time we are giving our customers to pay their bills. We can compare our DSO with that of others in our industry or region, or against the payment terms we have negotiated with our customers, to see how well we are managing our debtors.**

To see the exact amounts outstanding we would examine the aged debtors profile – the actual sums owed to us within 30, 60 or 90 days and any that are outstanding even longer than this.

Creditors (payables)

Supposing we buy and sell the same volume of goods, and get the same number of days of credit from our suppliers that we give to our customers. The amount of money we owe our suppliers should be less than that owed by our debtors (receivables). In other words, we expect to add some value between raw materials and the selling price for finished goods.

Thus, in Best we can see that with creditors (payables) exceeding debtors (receivables), their suppliers are funding the company's working capital.

A useful ratio to measure how effectively we are using this money to generate sales, is working capital as a percentage of sales. Working capital to sales is 14 per cent for Ace, 8 per cent for Best, 13 per cent for Cool, 20 per cent for Demon, 17 per cent for Excel, and 15 per cent for First. It should come as no surprise that Best performs well on this measure because of its high relative levels of creditors (payables).

Fixed assets

Fixed assets (for example, factory equipment and machinery) do not change in value from day to day, so managers cannot affect the asset value reported in the books except by buying and selling items. Hence, most management attention focuses on the other part of our asset base.

It is worth remembering that accountants value fixed assets at their book value, which is the purchase cost less depreciation, to take account of the reducing value of the assets as they wear out. It is normal to hold a fixed asset register which lists all the fixed assets a company owns and how they are depreciated to reflect the current book value.

Other assets

Although not mentioned in Table 5.2, companies often have other assets. An obvious example is cash. In large companies this is not included in a business unit's accounts as cash is usually managed centrally, and is therefore not necessarily available to that operation. It is also sometimes taken to the bottom of the balance sheet to offset short-term loans (eg an overdraft), thus reducing interest charges.

Goodwill

Finally, there are also intangible assets such as goodwill. This comes into play when a company buys another for more than the book value of the assets. The difference between what was paid and the book value of the assets is called goodwill. We can justify it any way we like, but to accountants goodwill is just the difference between these two numbers.

Asset turnover

Asset turnover is a measure of how effectively we are utilising all the money tied up in the business. It is calculated by dividing the sales from the P&L account by the net assets in the balance sheet. So, in our example the asset turnovers are: Ace: 2.9, Best: 3.4, Cool: 2.7, Demon: 2.6, Excel: 2.3 and First: 3.1. In other words, Best is working the money tied up in the business (its assets) the hardest. This is often referred to as 'sweating the assets', and people often think of this as getting those workers in the production plant to work harder. But really it's not those assets we can affect much on a day-to-day basis, compared to the working capital, which is often influenced by all the other departments as much as by production. Many companies operate well below their production capacity, in which case the way for them to improve their asset turnover is to raise sales volume, rather than just concentrate on production.

Return on net assets (RONA)

RONA is a measure of how much profit we are making on all the money invested in the business. It's a bit like asking, 'What return am I getting from the bank on the money I've got deposited?' In a business RONA is looking at the profit generated, compared with all the money that is tied up.

$$\text{Return on Net Assets} = \frac{\text{PBIT}}{\text{Net Assets}} \times 100\%$$

Ace has a RONA of 29 per cent, Best 34 per cent, Cool 32 per cent, Demon 29 per cent, Excel 23 per cent and First 28 per cent. So although Ace is making less absolute profit than Demon, it is making a similar level of profit for the money that is tied up in the business.

Gearing (leverage)

Gearing tells us how much of the company is really owned by the bank!

$$\text{Gearing} = \frac{\text{Loans}}{\text{Capital Employed}} \times 100\%$$

Capital employed is a common term for all the funds on the bottom half of the balance sheet and in UK accounting is the same as the top half of a balance sheet. Clearly, the lower the gearing, the less the company owes the bank and the greater the likelihood that it could borrow more money if required.

6

Getting finance from the bank

Introduction

The objective of this chapter is to provide a broad overview to securing bank finance. There are many detailed volumes written that can extend your knowledge if needed.

So you are setting up a new business or you have an existing business, but there is one thing you have in common – you need bank finance. Finance comes in many different forms. The more risk, the greater the potential reward to the lender.

While this chapter focuses on bank finance, it is worth setting out the broad principles of other sources as shown in table 6.1. Finance carries a cost; the equity cost is a share of ownership and future profits/losses, while bank finance cost comes in fees and interest. Late overdue tax payments can carry a penalty and extended trade credit may be negated by withdrawal of discounts for early settlement. The message – consider your options!

Table 6.1 Main types of finance

Risk factor for lender	Type of finance	Source	Explanation
Lowest risk	Bank debt	High street and other Banks provide funds that require repayment, plus interest. Usually accompanied by tangible security, either from the business assets, or the owners personal assets	The lowest risk because of the availability of security to cover the risk of failure
Medium risk	VAT, PAYE, National Insurance and Corporation Tax	Monies owed to 'the taxman' can be retained on extended terms, and by agreement, as a source of temporary finance. In times of economic uncertainty can be a very useful low cost source, at other times can be expensive carrying penal interest costs	Some priority is given in the event of failure for the payment of 'preferential creditors'
High risk	Trade credit	Credit given by suppliers helps finance the business, so the longer it is given the longer that finance is supporting the business. Often termed 'the cheapest form of credit' because it carries no cost	High risk because no security is available and in the event of default ranks behind the bank and the taxman

Highest risk	Equity or Share capital	Permanent investment in the business. Usually provided by the owners themselves (also known as shareholders), family and friends. Also from Business Angels & Venture Capital Funds	The highest risk as is the last creditor to be paid in the event of business failure

Your relationship with the bank

Life is about relationships; whether they are personal or business orientated. There is one thing in common – they always need careful consideration.

We have established you want some bank finance. Where do you go? Whom do you see? You could start by walking into your high street bank, or maybe not...

One of the oldest sayings is: 'It's not what you know, but who you know.' Never a truer word spoken. It is essential that you commence any bank relationship on the right footing, and it is critical that you avoid at all costs being 'turned down' by your bank – it is so hard to have a decision reversed in any walk of life.

So, make sure the relationship starts on the right basis. Ask yourself key questions about your knowledge of an individual in banking; do I know anyone? Can any of my contacts introduce me (and concurrently vouch for me)? My strongest advice would be to always seek a personal introduction from a friend, an accountant or solicitor you might know or another business colleague.

Later on in this chapter we will discuss maintaining that relationship, which is equally important.

Purpose of bank finance

When seeking Bank finance, there are two broad categories your requirement will fit into:

a)   Working Capital; that is to finance stock/raw material purchases or to provide the finance to allow customers to take extended credit ie to finance debtors.
b)   Capital Expenditure; that is the purchase of land and buildings, plant and machinery, investment in product development and/or growth requiring support in paying wages and buying materials ahead of launching that new product or indeed another business.

It is important to consider why you need to borrow money:

- **Working Capital is generally provided by short-term overdraft where your bank account fluctuates month by month between credit and debit.**
- **Working Capital can equally be provided by extending your trade credit, or negotiating delayed tax payments.**
- **Capital Expenditure is generally provided by long-term loans, repayable in monthly instalments.**
- **Capital Expenditure can equally be provided in other ways; for example the provision of a van could be financed by hire purchase, or taken on a lease agreement.**

Having established why you need to borrow, this will have an important bearing on how you present your plans to the bank.

Is your request viable?

A bank will only lend you money if it can reasonably expect to be repaid. You need to be able to show your ability to repay, whether it is a short-term overdraft or a longer term loan.

Some of what you need to cover is:

- **your track record;**
- **your historic results;**
- **a business plan (see below);**
- **last audited accounts;**
- **current and up-to-date management accounts;**
- **debtor and creditor lists;**
- **a budget for the current/next trading year;**
- **a cash flow forecast alongside the budget.**

The extent to which you can provide this information depends on whether you are a new 'start-up' business, or an established business that has been trading for many years and is seeking finance for the first time. However, consider this: even if you are a brand new business, you have a track record and historic results in your previous occupation that should be used to demonstrate your expertise and/or ability.

The detail of a business plan is widely misunderstood. It does not have to be a book. Indeed, it is better for all concerned if it isn't! Broadly it must cover 'your story' – how has the business come about; some detail about the product/services; the management of the business and its plans for the future; market research undertaken to support assumptions and forecasts; and the financial requirements.

The sum of this information should enable the reader to make a reasoned assessment on the viability of the proposition. Is the product right, does the market research support the budgeted sales, do the sums add up? Key will be does the business generate sufficient cash to repay its proposed borrowing from the bank?

A business is supplying various fashion chains and supermarkets with clothing. All the stock they purchase is done against confirmed purchase orders from their clients. All they have to do is have the stock manufactured to the correct specification and have it delivered on time. The bank looking at this scenario can make reasonable and safe judgements on their forecasts because they will be backed by confirmed purchase orders.

Categories of finance

a) **Working Capital:** This is to finance stock/raw material purchases or to provide the finance to allow customers to take extended credit ie to finance debtors. It is a revolving short-term facility over an agreed period of less than 12 months.

- *Overdraft:* where the bank allows your current account to 'go into negative' but would expect fluctuations between debit (overdrawn) and credit on a regular basis. The most flexible form of finance as little control is exercised by the bank – it can be used as is seen fit by the business. Interest is payable as well as an annual fee.

- *Invoice Discounting:* this is the borrowing of money against invoices or debtors that are due. Usually between 60 per cent and 80 per cent of the invoice value can be borrowed and incurs monthly fees plus interest, so is more expensive than an overdraft and is always restricted to how much your debtors owe. The most common form is Confidential Invoice Discounting, where your clients have no knowledge that you are borrowing against the money they owe you. The provider of this type of facility, often the bank's Invoice Finance Division, will carefully assess your client's credit worthiness on a regular basis.

- *Factoring:* very similar to Invoice Finance, but where the Invoice Finance provider also collects the debtor money from your client when due. This can be very attractive as it alleviates the need to have a Credit Controller chasing up overdue payments but can send out the wrong message about your cash flow position to the market.

b) **Capital Expenditure:** longer term finance required for the purchase of fixed assets or investment in the growth of the business. Can be made available for periods between 1 and 25 years where monthly repayments are made over the period of the loan to achieve full repayment. This can be achieved in several ways:
   – *Long-Term Loan:* the bank lends the money on agreed terms ie interest payments and set-up fees.
   – *Hire Purchase:* where the bank's Asset Finance Division will use the asset as security and advance the money to purchase that asset – commonly used for vehicle purchase.
   – *Leasing:* where the bank's Asset Finance Division retains ownership of the asset, leasing it to the client in exchange for a monthly/quarterly rental payment over the period of the agreement. At the end of the agreement, the asset is returned to the Asset Finance provider.

c) **The Enterprise Finance Guarantee Scheme (EFG):** this is worth a mention here because it is a relatively new UK government initiative to support small/medium-sized businesses. Loans of up to £1m are available over 10 years through the 'high street' bank network. A wide range of purposes are permitted with the government providing a guarantee to the bank instead of its normal security requirements. It is expensive because in addition to the fee and interest cost the bank will charge, a premium is payable to the government for the guarantee.

Securing your bank finance

Very rarely will a bank lend money without security. In the event of you defaulting it could recover its money by realising the value of any security pledged. There are misconceptions about what provides good security, so Table 6.2 sets out some principles.

A mortgage debenture is common company security giving a fixed and floating charge over all the assets of the business. It also gives the bank other rights, such as the appointment of an administrator, so careful consideration and professional advice should be taken.

Table 6.2 Types of security

Type of Security	Requirements
Freehold property	This will need to be valued by a bank-appointed valuer. If a mortgage already exists, and there is sufficient equity to allow a second mortgage, a further write-down is taken as a second charge offers less protection than the first charge.
Leasehold property	Must be with an unexpired lease greater than 21 years, otherwise the same criteria applies as above.
Government guarantee	Under EFG (see above), 75% of the amount borrowed is guaranteed by the government.
Stocks & shares	If offering a personal portfolio of investments, these should be broadly based. Market valuation is taken less a write-down for potential market volatility.
Plant & machinery*	Rarely provides good security, because often it is of a specialist nature. Alternatives to consider are Hire Purchase and Lease Finance, where an Asset Finance provider has greater expertise and control over the equipment.
Debtors*	Monies owing to the business offer a good alternative, but they must be widely based and current, ie not overdue and of good quality (which can be enhanced if they are insured). Always written down in value to allow for default, better 'value' is gained by use with an Invoice Finance facility (mentioned earlier).

Stock*	Rarely provides good security unless of a commodity nature. The issue is it must be readily saleable by the bank – it rarely is!
Personal guarantee	This is a promise to pay, if the business doesn't. You will be required to demonstrate personal wealth to support your pledge, and even provide those assets as security behind your guarantee.

*Commonly given through a Mortgage Debenture

Costs of borrowing

No borrower enjoys this aspect but it is a fact of life!

A lender earns their keep by charging a fee for setting up a facility, and interest for monies lent.

In addition there may be legal fees and valuation fees, if for example a property is being purchased, and also the cost of providing security documentation. Below are some examples of UK costs:

- **An overdraft will command an annual arrangement fee plus interest. Expect a minimum fee of 1 per cent of the gross limit, and 3 per cent above the bank's base rate.**
- **A long-term loan will attract perhaps a 2 per cent arrangement fee of the amount borrowed, plus a minimum interest rate of 2 per cent above the bank's base rate.**
- **The Enterprise Finance Guarantee Scheme will be priced as for a long-term loan, in addition to 2 per cent per annum payable to HM Treasury for provision of the government guarantee (although in 2009 there was a year 1 discount to 1.5 per cent).**
- **Invoice Discounting carries a set-up cost for an initial survey of the debtors of about £1,000, plus an annual fee of approximately 0.35 per cent of annual turnover**

(minimum commonly £500 per month), plus interest on the amount borrowed at a similar rate to an overdraft. The annual cost can be affected by the volume of debtors, and whether insurance is provided as part of the package.

- The cost of providing security documentation could be as low as £1,000, rising depending on the quantity, value and complexity involved.

Sources of help and support

There are a range of professional and other services available. The recommendations below are kept to a small focused list, as this subject could consume a book in its own right!:

- **The Institute of Chartered Accountants in England & Wales:** You can search their directory for a suitable accountant at http://www.icaewfirms.co.uk/
- **The National Association of Commercial Finance Brokers:** You can enlist the help of a specialist in securing finance at http://www.nacfb.org/
- **The Academy for Chief Executives:** a membership organisation where learning, support and advice is available at http://www.chiefexecutive.com/default.asp
- **Ecademy:** an online business network at http://www.ecademy.com/
- **Business Link:** a government sponsored organisation offering business advice at http://www.businesslink.gov.uk.

When should you apply for bank finance?

When should you approach the bank? The earlier the better, but not until you are ready! The test is: can you satisfy the requirements discussed earlier? Also, it is sometimes prudent to consider applying or refinancing when the business is looking particularly strong as there is more likelihood of your application being accepted.

In addition, you should be approaching the bank well ahead of your immediate need. It is not satisfactory to submit a proposition and demand an immediate answer – that is a sure way to receive bad news. Banks have processes of assessment to go through, and rarely will your manager be the sole decision maker. Some say that is a bad thing, but we believe it is good for customers to have an expert Credit Assessment of their proposition; if the bank supports you it believes in your proposal and that is good backing.

So, allow at least several working weeks for the bank to give a considered assessment and opinion on your proposal.

Maintaining the dialogue

It is important in any relationship to keep in touch. The main considerations are:

a) Ensure you comply with the terms of your facility. Often these will include the provision of monthly management accounts, and annual accounts within given timescales – simply ensure you do it!
b) Banks don't like surprises. If you have a problem, make sure you discuss it with your manager early. At least solutions can then be discussed, and there should be time to implement them. If you deliver bad news late in the day, almost as an ultimatum, don't count on the bank supporting you.
c) Communication is the key. Maintain good open lines of communication. Share the good news, make a telephone call when sending your management accounts in, have a regular visiting programme to suit your needs be it two, three or four times a year.

Arranging a facility and awaiting a reply from your bank is not the way to forge a strong relationship with a provider who should be considered a key supplier alongside other trade relationships. I am certainly not promoting 'wining and dining' as this is no longer appropriate or necessary, but your bank relationship should be soundly maintained by:

- **complying with information requests;**
- **good open lines of regular communication;**
- **paying a fair price for your facilities.**

Refinancing

Refinancing invariably means a change of bank. Otherwise you are simply renegotiating your existing terms.

In an environment of banks recapitalising, refinancing is probably one of the hardest tasks. The essential question is why would another bank want to take on somebody else's customer – what is wrong with the deal?!

Banks are very protective, and so if you are a sound client, with a good track record and a good proposition, why would your incumbent bank wish to let you move on?

The types of sound reason may be the following:

- **You wish to change banks because you receive poor day-to-day service.**
- **You wish to change bank because your bank manager is not experienced enough to understand the nature of your business.**
- **The bank is helping you to refinance because it wishes to exit your industry sector.**
- **The bank is helping you refinance because it is itself in difficulty and short of capital.**

Be realistic, and consider carefully your explanation when approaching another bank.

Summary

Prepare your proposal carefully and thoroughly. Provide all the information required by the bank, including:

- **your track record;**
- **your historic results;**
- **a business plan;**
- **last audited accounts;**
- **current and up-to-date management accounts;**
- **debtor and creditor lists;**
- **a budget for the current/next trading year;**
- **a cash flow forecast alongside the budget.**

Ensure you have considered the type of finance suitable, and built those assumptions into your plans, ie for an overdraft, that your cash flow shows fluctuations between credit and debt; for a loan that your cash flow shows repayments. Consider what security the bank might want, and the timing of your approach.

Last but not least, if you can, take professional advice and support in preparing and reviewing your proposal.

7

How our investors see us – stock market ratios

What accounts do our investors want to see?

If you were going to invest money in a company, what accounts would you want to see?

First, you would want to look at the P&L account. This would tell you what trading activity the company has had, what its costs are and whether it is profitable.

You would also want to see the balance sheet to see what assets the company has and how it is funded. You might also do some analysis using tools we have discussed earlier to decide if it is being run efficiently (eg by checking levels of working capital).

But we now know how important cash flow is for a business. In Chapter 5 we saw the cash flow forecast, but this is a tool for looking into the future. You can't imagine many companies wanting to publish such predictions about tomorrow! Investors still want to know something about cash – is the company generating or consuming cash? This leads to a third type of account – the cash flow statement (also known as funds flow).

Cash flow (funds flow) statement

The main elements of a cash flow statement are:

- **Cash flow from operations – This states how much cash is eventually going to be generated from sales less the costs of running the business. One thing to note here is that depreciation is added back in to the profit (which is only the sum of sales less costs), because as accountants would say, 'Depreciation is not a cash transaction' (see Chapter 10).**
- **Changes in working capital – Here we see whether we are consuming or generating cash by adjustments in our stocks, monies owed by customers (debtors) and the credit we get from suppliers (creditors). See Chapter 13 for more information.**
- **Changes in fixed assets and investments – Here we see whether we have bought or sold plant, equipment and investments in other companies, which would obviously have cash implications. We must not simply compare the current value of our assets on the balance sheet with a previous balance sheet, as the 'book value' of our assets will change because of depreciation, which has already been taken account of in the cash flow from operations above.**
- **Cash flow from financing – This examines if loans have been taken or paid off and the interest charges which will be paid out of cash.**

The sum of all these cash flows will determine whether overall the company is generating or consuming cash.

Shares

Let's look again at the six companies we were comparing in Chapter 5. These are shown again in Table 7.1.

Table 7.1 Stock market ratios – six companies

	Company					
	Ace	**Best**	**Cool**	**Demon**	**Excel**	**First**
Annual sales (£000)	100	120	150	160	180	200
Profit (earnings) (£000)	10	12	18	18	18	18
Share price (pence)	100	85	115	135	150	105
Issued share capital (£)	30,000	30,000	40,000	40,000	50,000	60,000
Total dividend (£000)	4	4	4	4	4	4
Earnings per share (EPS)	33	36	38	45	36	30
Price earnings ratio (P/E)	3	2.4	3	3	4.2	3.5

For an investor, which company is best? Most stock market ratios relate to items that must be published at least once per year, and this allows us to compare our performance with an industry average as a benchmark. These items are often published in the financial press along with details of the companies included in that industry group.

Ratios relating to shares

When a company is formed, the owners usually put some funds into the business to allow it to start trading. This is known as start-up capital. To denote what each owner has in the company a number of shares (or stock) are issued. These often have a notional face value rather than the full value of the funds put into the company by the owners.

Subsequently these shares may be traded on a public stock exchange. This process is known as an initial public offering (IPO) or stock market flotation. The price at which shares trade on a stock exchange bears little resemblance to the initial issued face value of the shares.

A share price moves every time a company's stock is traded, and represents the future expectations of those buying the shares. This is usually quoted in pence. If a company is expected to do well in the future then the share price will go up; if it is anticipated that it will do less well than in the past then the share price will go down. This can also extend to a whole industry even if your company is outperforming its competitors. Generally, the markets are only interested in how the price moves over time rather than some historic value (ie when the share was issued).

You may recall that a company ultimately operates to make a profit for its shareholders. As a shareholder I want to know how much of the profit a company makes belongs to me. By dividing the profit by the number of issued shares a ratio known as earnings per share (EPS) can be calculated (see Table 7.1).

A derivative of this ratio is the price/earnings ratio (P/E). We divide the share price by the EPS to calculate P/E (see Table 7.1). Only Excel and First exceed the industry average of 3.2.

What the ratio implies is that the share price is higher or lower for the current level of profit a company is delivering. So if the P/E is higher than the norm, there is an expectation that this company will do better in the future (hence the high share price), or perhaps the stock is overvalued for the current level of return.

Dividends

The level of profit (earnings) that a company makes is no indication of what cash payments a shareholder will actually receive. These payments depend upon a company's dividend policy. A dividend is usually a cash payment made to the shareholders. In the example above, all the companies are paying the same overall amount of dividends (£4,000 per year) but there are a different number of issued shares in each company. Therefore, the actual dividend per share for Ace and Best is 13, Cool and Demon 10, Excel 8 and First 7. Dividends per share are normally quoted in pence.

Occasionally a company will give shareholders a non-cash dividend in the form of new shares (or stock). This is known as a scrip dividend.

The yield of a share is the dividend value per share, expressed as a percentage of the share price. The yield for Ace is 13 per cent, Best 15 per cent, Cool 9 per cent, Demon 7 per cent, Excel 5 per cent and First 7 per cent. You can imagine the yield as being like the interest rate you would be getting from a bank, for the money you have invested in that company's stock. In this case, against an industry average of 9 per cent Best is ahead on this metric.

Over a period of years, most industries establish a norm in terms of the dividends paid out to the shareholders. Generally, the lower the risk of an industry, the more that is paid out as dividend and the less retained in the business. So, for instance, in the chemical industry it is common to pay half of the net profit generated by the company as dividends and retain the rest for future growth. A biotechnology company may never pay a dividend, as it is accepted by the shareholders that any profit should be left in the company to fund future research.

Market capitalisation

Lastly, the value of a company can be ascertained by multiplying the number of issued shares by the current share price. This is known as market capitalisation. The market capitalisation for Ace is 30,000, Best 25,500, Cool 46,000, Demon 54,000, Excel 75,000 and First 63,000. This represents what it might cost to buy all the shares in a company.

In reality, if one company wants to take over another, it must buy all the shares in that company. Clearly, shareholders will want a higher price than the share is currently trading at, or they will not want to sell their shares to this other company. This is called the share premium. In a hostile takeover the shareholders are approached directly by the company wanting to buy, rather than on the recommendation of the directors (who were appointed by the shareholders to run the company on their behalf).

Valuing a company

How much should you pay for a business? Let's consider the same six companies again (see Table 8.1).

How should we put a value on what these companies are worth? There is only one accurate answer to this question – whatever someone is prepared to pay! In evaluating 'worth' we must consider a number of alternatives.

Below are many examples of financial measures but we must never forget the non-financial measures which are discussed in the Balanced Scorecard measure outlined later. These factors can far outweigh any financial appraisal, as it is only based on a company's past track record rather than its future potential.

When putting a value on a company, always consider more than one measure, to allow a 'reality check' on the methods being used.

Asset value

An obvious starting point for valuing a company is to look at the asset base of that organisation. On this basis the companies above

Table 8.1 Valuing six companies

	Company					
	Ace	**Best**	**Cool**	**Demon**	**Excel**	**First**
Annual sales (£000)	100	120	150	160	180	200
Profit (earnings) (£000)	10	12	18	18	18	18
Net assets (£000)	34	43	55	62	77	65
Share price (pence)	100	85	115	135	150	105
Issued share capital (£)	30,000	30,000	40,000	40,000	50,000	60,000

would be worth their net asset value. There are some limitations to this approach:

- **Book value** – Accountants usually value fixed assets at what they cost, depreciated to reflect the reducing value as items are worn out in use. Book value may not be an accurate reflection of the real value. This can apply when land and buildings were bought some time ago, and have grown in value; or if the value of these assets has reduced significantly since purchase, due to new technologies. There may also be a factor that has previously been ignored, such as environmental issues. Disposal or land remediation costs could wipe out any asset value.

  Normally a company will have a fixed asset register that lists all its assets, and the current depreciated book value of those assets. A similar register might also exist for its other assets (see below).

- **Working capital** – Again, we must understand whether these items are accurately stated. Stock (inventory) is usually valued by accountants at what it cost. This may be far more than we can sell it for, especially if it is out of date. Debtors (receivables) is money owed to us by customers. How much of this might be bad debt (ie invoices that may never get paid)? Creditors (payables) is money we owe our suppliers. How much has our company avoided paying to improve its cash flow?
- **Intangible assets** – This can take the form of goodwill (the difference between what we pay for an acquisition and what the assets are valued at) or capitalised costs (such as research or start-up costs). As there are no physical assets to underwrite these, the net assets may be overstated if these elements are high.
- **Investments** – There might be some investments in other companies, which accountants will value at what was paid for them, rather than their realisable value in the market.
- **Unstated assets** – Accountants usually put no value in the books on such things as people, brands, intellectual property, market position, forward order book etc. This means that the net asset figure alone might seriously understate the company value. This can apply especially in service-based businesses that have few tangible assets.

Multipliers

Another simple approach is to use a multiplier to calculate a company's value. These multipliers will vary for different industries. One way of deciding what figure to pick for a multiplier is to analyse previous company takeovers within that sector, examining what was paid for these businesses compared to their sales or profit levels.

Caution must be taken in ensuring that the level of sales or profits in the accounting period being analysed is sustainable and does not contain one-off or abnormal conditions.

Sales multiplier

The sales multiplier uses a multiple of sales to assign a value to that company. This could be less than or greater than 1, depending on expectations for future growth. Sales multipliers are particularly popular in start-up companies that are not yet profitable (eg dot.com companies).

Profit multiplier

In the case of the profit multiplier, the multiplier used tends to be greater than 1 and will be based on how many years' future profit are to be factored into the value of a business as well as expectations for future profit growth.

So if a profit multiplier of 10 was used you might expect a 10 per cent return for the next 10 years, with no change in business conditions to pay for this investment.

Market capitalisation

As mentioned in Chapter 7, the value of a company can be ascertained by multiplying the number of issued shares by the current share price. This is known as market capitalisation.

A case for asset stripping?

We can use the information from the case study above to do the financial analysis shown in Table 8.2.

The concept of asset stripping is to buy out a company's shares for less than the value of the assets and then to sell

> these at a profit. Best might therefore be a candidate for this treatment based on these calculations.
>
> This is why company directors get worried when their share price falls too low!

Table 8.2 Analysing the case for asset stripping

	Company					
	Ace	**Best**	**Cool**	**Demon**	**Excel**	**First**
Net assets (£)	34,000	43,000	55,000	62,000	77,000	65,000
Sales multiplier (×1.5)	150,000	180,000	225,000	240,000	270,000	300,000
Profit multiplier (×4)	40,000	48,000	72,000	72,000	72,000	72,000
Market capital-isation (£)	30,000	25,500	46,000	54,000	75,000	63,000

Balanced Scorecard

As already mentioned, there are often non-financial considerations to valuing a company. Norton and Kaplan developed the idea of a scorecard that balances financial and non-financial measures, to help manage a company; but these ideas can also help us value one. Non-financial measures might include:

- Health, safety and environment – many companies have policies relating to these factors and would seek an acquisition that might enhance their position in these areas. This could include accident rates, environmental impact and energy usage.
- Production measures – these will vary from one industry to another but might include production efficiencies, output per worker, waste levels and how up to date the production processes are.
- Intellectual property – the potential value of patents, trademarks and brands.
- Employees – the skills, motivation, satisfaction levels, productivity and loyalty of the people who work in the company.
- Marketing – geographic coverage, customer satisfaction and loyalty, market share and potential fit with existing activities have a value that can be different for different purchasers. The outlook for future growth might lead to an expectation of a better performance in the future, as could the rate of product and process innovation, and percentage of sales from new products.
- Strategic fit – difficult to quantify, and used to justify high acquisition costs! Companies will also claim to be able to gain synergies and cost savings through merging the two organisations.

Cash flows

When considering purchasing a company, another way to value the business is to examine what cash it will generate over a period of time. This can be in straight cash terms not taking into account inflation, price erosion etc. You may also wish to apply discounted cash flow principles (see Chapter 13) to arrive at a net present value (NPV) for the company, or even an internal rate of return (IRR) on the purchase.

Perhaps the most useful way to value it is to estimate the economic profits that the business will generate in the next few years (see Chapter 9) and then apply the NPV process to them. All valuations based on forecast figures are essentially educated guesses, but this analysis is likely to pinpoint the best opportunity for creating value, if the forecasts turn into reality.

9

Shareholder value and economic profit

Shareholders invest in a company to make a profit. This can come from an increase in the share price and/or the dividends the company pays. Both share prices and dividends have been discussed in detail in Chapter 7. The challenge is to find a measure of business performance that correlates with share price movements. Then, if we plan our business to raise this measure, we should raise the share price, and hence create value for our shareholders.

Earnings before interest, tax, depreciation and amortisation (EBITDA)

Profit is not a good measure of the value a business is generating for its shareholders. Ultimately, a shareholder is interested in the amount of cash generated, rather than profit (which is after all only an accounting calculation). It is cash which enables the business to expand and develop, and pay dividends. And it is the expectation of future cash flows that drives the share price up, and creates values for shareholders.

In calculating profit, depreciation is included as a cost.

Depreciation and amortisation are not cash transactions but an accounting exercise to balance the reducing value of assets over time. We can measure earnings before interest, tax, depreciation and amortisation – EBITDA! This is the amount of operating profit that will eventually be turned into cash. But EBITDA alone doesn't tell us if we are creating value.

Economic profit

Economic profit (EP)[1] takes account of the fact that investors have choices. They can invest in your company, or your competitor; in art; in another industry; or put their money in the bank. Every investment has a certain amount of risk, and a level of reward.

If your company generates more cash from each pound invested than other investments with a similar level of risk, it is making an 'economic profit'. Studies of real companies show clearly that an increase in EP correlates strongly with an increase in share price, and the creation of shareholder value. A fall in EP goes with a reduction in share price, and destruction of shareholder value.

Economic profit is calculated by taking the cash flow generated by the business (EBITDA) and subtracting a 'charge' for the 'cost of capital'. The cost of capital is the profit the business must make, simply to meet the expectations of investors who take this level of risk.

If the company was financed only by shareholders' funds, the cost of capital would be the average return of investments after tax with the same level of risk; for example, a group of companies of similar size in the same industry. This is the 'cost of equity'.

---

[1] EP is also known as economic value added (EVA®), net contribution to value (NCV) and shareholder value added (SVA). EVA® is a registered trademark of the Stern Stewart Corporation.

Most companies are financed partly by shareholders' funds, and partly by bank loans. So, their cost of capital is not simply the cost of equity, but takes into account the interest paid on loans as well. This is known as the 'weighted average cost of capital', or the WACC rate.

Economic profit is calculated by subtracting a capital charge (the net asset value of a business multiplied by the WACC rate) from EBITDA. Tax is also deducted because this is paid out of cash flow. Interest is not deducted, as the capital charge has already taken this into account.

Thus, in the example shown in Table 9.1, while Cool's profits are in line with those of several of the other companies, it is creating more value (over and above the cost of the money tied up in that business) than its competitors.

Table 9.1 Economic profit = Profit – Tax – Capital charge

£	Company					
	Ace	**Best**	**Cool**	**Demon**	**Excel**	**First**
Profit (earnings)	10,000	12,000	18,000	18,000	18,000	18,000
Tax (33%)	3,300	4,000	6,000	6,000	6,000	6,000
Net assets	34,000	35,000	55,000	62,000	77,000	65,000
Capital charge (10% WACC rate)	3,400	3,500	5,500	6,200	7,700	6,500
Economic profit	3,300	4,500	6,500	5,800	4,300	5,500

Total shareholder return (TSR)

Recently, economists have come up with a further measure of returns for the shareholder. While profits are owned by the shareholders, they are not necessarily paid out as dividends, and may be retained in the business to fund its growth. For instance, biotech companies often do not pay a dividend to their shareholders.

In reality the return a shareholder sees is the increase in the share price over time, and the cash dividends received from the company. Typically this TSR is normally calculated over the past three to five years.

This can be further complicated by using discounted cash flow to reflect the fact that money earned in the future is worth less than its worth today. TSR calculated in this way is used by a number of companies, but there is little evidence that the stock markets have adopted this as a measure of shareholder value over more conventional measures such as the share price and profit performance.

Recently, Unilever used this concept and concluded that making a cash distribution represented better shareholder value than retaining it in the business for future growth. On making this payment the share price collapsed, because economists had forgotten the psychological effect this payout would make. Shareholders said, 'Thanks for the bonus, I'm not likely to get a payout like that again, I'll invest the money somewhere else!' and all tried to sell their shares. Strangely, a short time later Unilever borrowed money to make an acquisition and the share price went up again as investors believed the company would be able to make better profits in the future as a result of better use of this funding.

A drawback of looking at TSR is that we are either looking at historic performance over the last three to five years (which is not necessarily an indication of future trends) or we are estimating future values (say, for the share price) which are not always borne out in practice.

10

The hidden costs – depreciation, amortisation and tax

Depreciation and amortisation are financial conventions used to take account of the fact that assets reduce in value over time. In some cases, such as vehicles, they simply wear out, even if they are well maintained. In other cases, such as software, they may become obsolete, and need to be replaced even though they work perfectly. This can happen simply because there is now a better product available, and the cost of using the old one is much higher than the cost of using the new one. So, accountants have to estimate the useful life of an asset when it is bought, using their best judgement. If they overestimate this, the asset may be worthless while it still shows as an asset on the books. On the other hand, some assets outlive their expected working life, and still have real value many years later, but don't appear on the balance sheet any more.

The depreciation and amortisation is the amount by which the assets are reduced in value during each accounting period. This is taken as a charge in the P&L, as a fixed cost or expense.

We have already established that assets are normally valued by accountants at what they cost, and this is known as the book value of the asset. This book value then reduces by the amount that the asset is depreciated or amortised over time.

Land and buildings are not normally depreciated in the United Kingdom, as they are not 'worn out' in use. However, in recent times where land and buildings become contaminated, the remediation costs may drastically reduce their value.

This chapter outlines the concepts of depreciation and amortisation, but every company has its own policies, so you should ask your financial staff to explain how these operate in your own company.

Generally it is becoming accepted practice that depreciation is used for tangible assets (physical items such as cars, computers, equipment etc) and amortisation for intangible assets (goodwill, capitalised costs etc – explained later). Remember that both depreciation and amortisation are accounting conventions to take account of the reducing value of assets. Because something changes on the top half of the balance sheet, we must make an adjustment to the bottom half. This is done by reducing the profit carried across the page from the P&L account by the amount of the depreciation and amortisation. This is only a paper exercise – the cash in the bank does not change as a result of this adjustment in the value of the assets and so accountants will tell you, 'This is not a cash transaction' – it has no impact on cash.

Depreciation

There are two main methods for calculating depreciation. First, an assumption has to be made of the economic life of an asset. So, for instance, a car may be depreciated over four years, while a computer might be depreciated over two years, and production equipment over 10 or 20 years.

Most companies have a depreciation policy set by their finance department. One organisation depreciates its plant and equipment over 17 years – and no one seems to know why at some point in the company's history this figure was selected!

Straight line depreciation

The first method of depreciation is called straight line depreciation and reduces the value of the asset by an equal amount for each period throughout its life (see Figure 10.1). So, if an asset has an original value of 100 and has a useful life of 10 years, the depreciation would be 10 per year using this approach. After 10 years the asset will have a zero book value and can no longer be depreciated. This is known as a fully depreciated asset.

The advantage of this method is its simplicity. The disadvantage is the fact that at some point the asset has no book value, which does not necessarily reflect the real situation. This can be a problem when a business has become accustomed to a

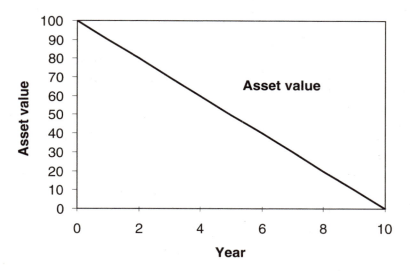

Figure 10.1   Straight line depreciation

level of profit without any depreciation charges, from a fully depreciated manufacturing asset. As soon as any capital improvements are made to the equipment the business will have depreciation charges from these improvements, and profit will reduce for no apparent reason.

So, for instance, when some smart young engineer comes along and wants to automate the plant, profits could go down! That said, perhaps the automation would reduce fixed costs (fewer workers may mean a lower wage bill), thus offsetting the new depreciation charges.

Reducing balance depreciation

Alternatively, the value of an asset can be reduced by a set percentage each period (see Figure 10.2). So, for the example above, the percentage used would be 10 per cent based on a 10-year life. Each year the value of the asset is reduced by 10 per cent, but after 10 years the asset will still have some residual book value. Each year the amount of depreciation reduces and neither the depreciation nor the book value of the asset ever becomes zero.

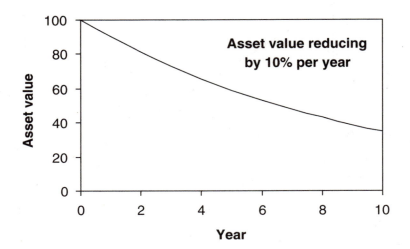

Figure 10.2 Reducing balance depreciation

The advantage of this method is the fact that the asset usually has some residual value even at the end of its useful life, and this is reflected in the final book value. The disadvantage is the complexity of managing many different assets at different stages in their life, and the ever-changing amount of depreciation, which affects the profits of a company.

It is because fixed assets are valued at their depreciated 'book value' that it is so important for a company to maintain a fixed asset register (mentioned elsewhere in this book).

Goodwill

Goodwill is simply the difference between what is paid for an asset and its book value. It usually comes into consideration when a company makes an acquisition. There are many reasons for paying more than the book value for an asset. First, the book value of an asset in the accounts may not reflect its true market value. For instance, land and buildings may be valued in the books at what was paid for them (historic value), even if this was many years before, and their value may have changed significantly.

When buying a business that is already established, there are many intangible aspects such as the staff (which you will recall accountants put no value on, except for instance in football clubs), market position, brands, technology and intellectual property, which all have a value. This might help to explain why Nestlé paid many times the value of the production assets to acquire the Rowntree confectionery company, which included the global brands Kit-Kat and Smarties, neither of which were valued on Rowntree's balance sheet.

Goodwill is treated as an intangible asset and is placed on the balance sheet as a separate item from the tangible assets. Companies must decide whether to carry the goodwill indefinitely, amortise goodwill over a number of years, write it off against profits immediately, or revalue the assets. What is this intangible asset? It does not physically exist; it is just the difference between what is paid for an asset and its value in the books (on the balance sheet).

Intangible assets

Companies will often acquire and develop items that are not physical materials. This can include such things as trademarks, intellectual property (eg patents) and brands, customised software, databases and market research information. Accountants tend only to put a value on tangible assets such as buildings and equipment.

> Accountants argue that these other assets are somewhat transient. Consider the Perrier water brand. This was the number one branded bottled water before the problem the company had with contaminated bottles. When the company had to withdraw all its stock from the shops, the value of the brand dramatically declined. It was only by considerable efforts in both rebranding and launching new products that Perrier has been able to re-establish its market position.

So, accountants define as intangible any asset on the balance sheet that has been paid for, but is not a physical item. Such assets have to be on the balance sheet because we have taken one item – cash – and turned it into another – an intangible asset. Without this being listed, the books would no longer balance.

As mentioned earlier, these intangible assets can be reduced in value over time by amortisation, in just the same way that tangible assets (eg equipment) are depreciated over time. Below is a further example of use of this mechanism with the capitalisation of costs.

Capitalising costs

Consider a pharmaceutical company that has to pay £400 million to research a new drug. Normal accounting convention would suggest that all development costs must be taken in the P&L account as they occur. In this case, it would be before any sales of the new drug had even taken place.

Companies capitalise costs so that they can match that cost with the timing of the sales income stream. The initial cost (£400 million in the pharmaceutical company example) is put on the balance sheet as an intangible asset, and then amortised in the same way as depreciation over the life of the project. If the life of the patented drug was 10 years from launch, the pharmaceuticals company might take an amortisation charge of £40 million per year over the life of the patent, following the launch of the drug. In this way it matches the research costs in the P&L account with the sales activity of the drug.

The downside of this technique is that whether the drug succeeds or fails, the amortisation costs remain. So, if the drug were withdrawn and had no further sales, a decision would have to be made whether to continue the amortisation charge each year, or write off the remaining value of the research from the balance sheet as one single charge in the P&L account.

Examples of items that might be capitalised include research, design and development costs, start-up and commissioning costs, refurbishment and overhaul costs, product launch costs and promotional campaigns. In principle, any cost which benefits the business for more than 12 months could be capitalised.

Taxation

Of the two certainties in life, it is sometimes debatable which is the worse to contemplate – death or taxes. The complexities of the tax system can bring grown men to tears, let alone what it does to their profits. After depreciation, more people probably get confused about tax than any other aspect of the accounts. It certainly deserves a brief and simple review. This is based on a UK company. We will have a quick look at value added tax (VAT), income tax (Pay As You Earn, PAYE), National Insurance (NI) and corporation tax.

VAT

Put very simply, we charge customers VAT on most sales and we pay suppliers VAT on most purchases. At the end of each quarter we pay Customs and Excise the balance, or claim it from Customs and Excise if we have made more purchases than sales that attract VAT. You might think that claiming back VAT is a good thing, until you realise what it means – you are buying more than you are selling.

Indeed, a large VAT bill is a healthy sign; it means not only that you are selling more than you are buying, but that the difference in value is big – you are adding value, hence the name. The only problem is that it can knock your cash flow for six.

VAT can be a nightmare for people still doing their accounts manually, though in principle the record of VAT is no more than another column in the sales and purchase ledgers. Modern software makes it very easy. When entering each transaction the appropriate VAT code is nominated and the computer does the rest. At the quarter end, at the press of a button the machine tells you how much you owe, or how much to claim.

We said above that we charge customers VAT on most sales and we pay suppliers VAT on most purchases. There are exceptions to this, and without going into it in great detail, here are a few examples:

- **There are a few purchases that are not subject to VAT, eg books, some printed materials, travel, insurance, food (but not from restaurants) and children's clothes.**
- **There are some suppliers who are not big enough, in turnover terms, to have to charge VAT. They are not VAT registered.**
- **If goods or services are delivered in the EU, VAT does not have to be charged so long as the supplier is in possession of the client's VAT registration number. There are some complexities around this but the general statement is correct.**
- **If goods or services are supplied outside the EU, VAT is not applicable.**

It is important to realise that VAT does not feature in, or affect in any way, the P&L account. The only effect it has on the running of the business involves cash flow. If a company is trading mainly in the one country and has sold more than it has purchased (ie added value), a bill is building up, and when it is due to be paid the cash has to be found.

A business that forgets this fact is in for a nasty surprise. Small businesses in particular, and those in the catering trades more than any other, fall foul of this lapse of memory. Ever wondered why that nice little restaurant that opened up a little while back just closed and went overnight? It could be that their first VAT bill arrived.

Pay As You Earn (PAYE) and National Insurance (NI)

Most people know enough about PAYE and NI as they affect their incomes. Many do not know about employer's NI, or realise that on all salaries, bonuses etc the company pays about 12 per cent extra NI that the employee never sees. There is also a complex employer's NI situation with regard to company cars and other benefits – another hidden cost to the company.

When the salaries and wages are shown in the P&L they are gross figures including all PAYE and NI paid by employees and employers.

Corporation tax

Again viewed very simply, at the end of a financial year when a company has made a profit, corporation tax is due to be paid. The rate is in the region of 20–25 per cent (depending on the size of the company etc) and the cash has to be handed over to the Inland Revenue about nine months after the end of the financial year. Great, you get to hang on to it for nine months, but be very certain that you don't forget – the shock of this one to your cash flow can be terminal.

If a company makes a loss then no tax is due and in principle the loss can be used to offset taxable profit in other years.

11

What must we sell to make a profit?

We are about to consider a tool known as a break-even analysis, but before we do this we need to clarify some more bits of terminology. The break-even analysis deals with costs, split by accountants into what they call 'fixed' and 'variable'. Don't try applying the dictionary definitions of these words; we must remember that accountants use words in some strange ways. However, it is well worth getting to grips with what they *do* mean by these words, as the resultant tool is very powerful.

Variable costs

Accountants define a variable cost as one that behaves as shown in Figure 11.1.

Variable costs increase in proportion to units sold. A vital 'acid test' of a truly variable cost is one where, if there are no sales, you have no costs reported in the P&L account.

A good example of this involves raw materials. The cost of these goods is only reported in the P&L account when they are sold, not when purchased, or indeed converted into saleable finished goods.

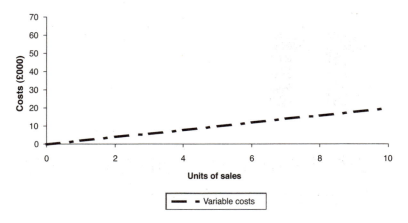

Figure 11.1 Variable costs

When is a cost a cost?

If you buy raw materials from which to manufacture your own product, then the cost of those materials is not registered on the P&L until your product is sold. This is true of any variable cost, a cost that is proportional to the volume of sales. If you make no sales in a year, the P&L will show no variable costs.

But, of course, you have paid for these materials, with real cash, so they have to be registered somewhere – entered on the balance sheet. The balance sheet will show these materials as an asset, under 'stocks'.

Clearly, there is a cost to this stock, but it appears in the balance sheet and is only realised into the P&L account when you sell it. Further examples of variable costs are packaging (for distribution to customers), freight (to customers), commissions and import/export duties.

If in doubt about whether a cost is variable, ask yourself, 'Does this cost go up the more I sell, and if I sell nothing do I have no costs (in the P&L account)?' If it does not meet these criteria, it is not a variable cost.

Fixed costs

Beware – the accountant defines a fixed cost as anything that is not a variable cost! In other words, if it does not meet the criteria above, it is a fixed cost. This is a prime example of confusing jargon, where words don't mean what they appear to; your advertising bill may go up and down, month by month, but it is a fixed cost. The unit cost of your raw materials may be stable for years on end, but raw materials will be a variable cost. Figure 11.2 is a graph showing fixed costs.

Fixed costs only behave like this over a limited range of values – for instance, rent may be the same whether you have an office full or empty, but if you need to rent a second office to hold more staff, the rent will go up to a new 'fixed' level.

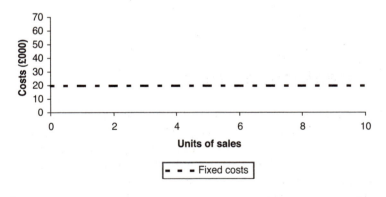

Figure 11.2 Fixed costs

Controllable/non-controllable costs

There are two categories of fixed costs: those that really are fixed (for the moment, in any case) and those that might vary. Accountants call the first group non-controllable or non-discretionary costs. The fixed costs that might vary, or, as an accountant would prefer to say, those that can be managed, are termed controllable or discretionary. Examples of discretionary costs include promotion, overtime, additional storage, temporary staff costs, maintenance, research and development, and training. These costs can be managed – we have choices about whether to spend this money or not.

Non-controllable costs are those we incur irrespective of sales activity and include wages, heating and lighting, rent, lease costs and breakdown maintenance.

> **Because the term 'fixed' implies that you cannot change this cost, Americans prefer to use the term 'expenses'. We all know that you can manage expenses whereas there can be a mental block about reducing things which are 'fixed'!**

Break-even point

Once we have determined our fixed and variable costs we can plot a break-even chart as shown in Figure 11.3.

Notice that in constructing this graph we stack the variable costs on top of the fixed costs such that this line now represents total costs. Finally, we plot a line showing sales income at a given price (in this example it is £7,000 per unit).

Having constructed the chart, we must now make sense of it. First, where the sales income line crosses the total cost line is our break-even point. In this case it is at four units. If our capacity were just six units you can see that all the profit is made on the last two

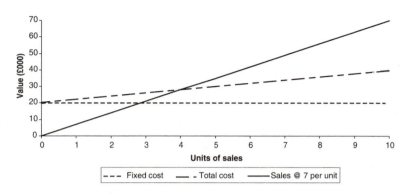

Figure 11.3 Break-even chart

units we sell. The first four units simply cover our costs, and once we have done this, anything more we sell generates us a profit.

Drawing a break-even chart also allows you to understand the key financial levers driving your business, as the two examples below demonstrate.

High fixed costs

Once you've created a break-even chart, the first thing to do is to compare the level of fixed costs with the variable costs and decide which is the bigger. So, for instance, in the example shown in Figure 11.4 is quite clear that the fixed costs are very much higher than the variable costs. This could be the situation in a bulk manufacturing business where the raw material costs are quite low compared to the costs of wages, depreciation, maintenance, sales and technical support etc.

In this case, shown below, the break-even point is now just below seven units. Every additional unit sees a huge jump in profit. At seven units we generate a profit of £2,000. An extra unit of sales (14 per cent increase in sales) produces a huge 300 per cent improvement in profit to £8,000. Thus, if your fixed costs exceed your variable costs, volume is a key driver for your business, and control of your fixed costs is also critical.

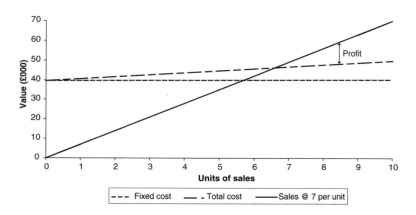

Figure 11.4 Break-even chart – high fixed costs

High variable costs

If your variable costs are significantly higher than your fixed costs, your break-even chart might look like the example shown in Figure 11.5. This might occur if you are buying in finished goods and reselling them, or you act as a distributor for others. In this way you only really incur major costs when you make a sale (as, for instance, with a travel agent, who only has the cost of a holiday if they sell you the trip).

The dynamic of the business shown in Figure 11.5 is very different to that in the earlier example. If we discount our selling price by just 7 per cent from £7,000 per unit to £6,500 we must sell almost three units more (a 60 per cent increase in sales) just to cover our costs. So, if your variable costs exceed your fixed costs then price is a key driver for your business, and so is control of your variable costs.

For this type of business, we must look beyond the obvious variable costs of production. Often it is sales commissions, credit card collection fees, insurance or freight charges that can have a big impact on overall profitability. Small improvements to these costs can make a big difference to the bottom line. This explains

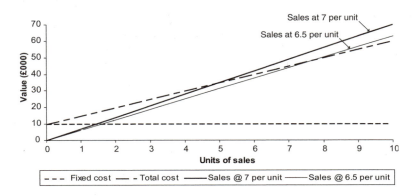

Figure 11.5 Break-even chart – high variable costs

why companies like easyJet charge for credit card payments, telephone bookings etc.

Uses of a break-even chart

The construction of a break-even chart is just the first step. In managing a business for better profits the graph suggests four options:

- **Reduce fixed costs.**
- **Reduce variable costs.**
- **Increase selling price.**
- **Increase volume of sales.**

While all these options will have an impact on the bottom line, which of these actions is most effective depends on the dynamic of your business. You can test the sensitivity of your business to each parameter to understand the key drivers for your profitability.

The break-even chart also provides a ready reckoner for what percentage of your business covers your costs, and how much safety margin you have. In other words, how much volume of sales can you lose, and still stay profitable?

Or, if your prices come under pressure from competitors, how low can you let them go, and still make the profit you want to achieve?

12

Tools for evaluating projects

When considering investing in a project, it is important to bear in mind that money to be had sometime in the future is not worth as much as the same money held today. This is not just about inflation, or interest rates, but also about what else the money could be invested into, making a return for you.

So, if we had £100 to invest today at a return of 30 per cent, Table 12.1 shows how we might expect it to grow in value if we continued to reinvest the full sum of money year after year. By Year 6, our £100 would have grown in value to £371.

This disparity in the value of money is known as the opportunity cost, or why the 'bird in the hand' really is 'worth two in the bush'... We will now examine a number of tools for making our calculations a little more precise than that!

Table 12.1 Investing £100 at 30 per cent return

	Year					
Growth at 30%	**1**	**2**	**3**	**4**	**5**	**6**
Value of investment	100	130	169	220	286	371

Payback

Suppose you could invest in a project with the cash flows shown in Table 12.2.

Thus, if you were to make the initial investment of £150,000 in Year 1, not only would you recover this, but in cash terms you would generate £250,000 on top of this by Year 6. The payback is the time it takes to recover the investment purely in cash terms. In this case it would be two and a half years (ie at Year 3.5).

Discounted cash flow (DCF)

We now have to consider what to discount the cash by to reflect the fact that money earned in the future is worth less than cash today because of the opportunity cost. Let's assume that we could get a 30 per cent return on money we invested in our business. The discount rate that we will therefore use for this example is 30 per cent.

To discount the cash flows, we must first calculate a discount factor to apply in each year of the cash flows. For instance, in Year 2, £100 would be worth 100/130 times its initial value – £77 in Year 1's money. This assumes that if we had the money in Year 1 we could invest it at 30 per cent so that by Year 2 it was worth £100. In Year 3 £100 would be worth £77 times 100/130, or £59 in Year 1's money, and so on.

The DCF would look like that shown in Table 12.3.

Note that DCF is a series of figures over a period of time discounted at a particular rate to reflect opportunity costs.

Table 12.2 Cash flows showing payback

£000	Year					
	1	2	3	4	5	6
Cash flows	(150)	50	50	100	100	100
Cumulative cash flows	(150)	(100)	(50)	50	150	250

Table 12.3 Discounted cash flow

Discount rate 30%				Year		
£000	1	2	3	4	5	6
Cash flows	(150)	50	50	100	100	100
Discount factor (100/130)	1.00	0.77	0.59	0.46	0.35	0.27
Discounted cash flow	(150)	39	30	46	35	27
Cumulative discounted cash flow	(150)	(111)	(81)	(35)	0	27

Net present value (NPV)

By adding up the DCF we arrive at a figure of £27,000 in Year 6. This means that not only will the project make a 30 per cent return (the amount by which we have discounted the cash flows), but in Year 6 it will generate cash of £27,000 in today's money. This cumulative DCF is known as net present value (NPV).

NPV is the sum of a series of cash flows over a given number of years, discounted at a particular rate to reflect opportunity cost. When comparing NPVs from several projects, remember to check the discount rate applied, and the number of years of cash flows taken into account.

Internal rate of return (IRR)

The internal rate of return of a project is the discount rate which must be applied to reach an NPV of zero in a given number of years. Thus the IRR for the above project after five years is 30 per cent – the discount rate used to get an NPV in Year 5 of zero.

If a discount rate of less than 30 per cent had been used, the NPV in Year 5 would be greater than zero. Equally, if a rate higher than 30 per cent had been used, the NPV would still be negative in Year 5.

An important consideration when comparing IRRs between projects is to be aware of the number of years of cash flows that is being used in the calculation.

Lastly, there is a concept called modified internal rate of return (MIRR). A flaw in using IRR is that it assumes that you can reinvest positive cash flows at the same internal rate of return. This is not always true. MIRR allows you to set a rate that the model uses to reinvest these positive cash flows.

Terminal values

As can be seen from the discounted cash flow example, money earned in the future is worth less and less in today's money as time goes on. At some point, money earned in the future is worth nothing in today's currency. Thus, there are calculations that can be done (or produced on a spreadsheet) which consider the terminal value of a project if it continues to generate the same cash flow year after year into the future.

Economic profit

An alternative approach for evaluating a project is to consider the economic profit generated over its life. To do this, a charge is taken for the capital tied up in the project. This may include the fixed assets purchased *and* the additional working capital (ie additional stock, debtors and creditors) created in doing the project.

We take this capital charge and any resultant taxation from the operating profit generated by the project to arrive at the economic profit in a similar way to that described in Chapter 9. These economic profits, generated each year through the life of the project, could then be discounted as above to reach an NPV for the economic profit in today's money.

Pitfalls

It can be dangerous to rely on figures produced for you, without knowing a little background to the project being appraised. Here are some thoughts:

- **How reliable are the cash flow forecasts?**
- **What timescale has been assumed for the project and why? Is there a sales contract life that can be used?**
- **Have inflation, exchange rates and future changes in costs been taken into account in calculating project cash flows?**
- **What pricing and volume assumptions lie behind income streams?**
- **What discount rate has been used and why?**

Clearly, all these factors can influence the numbers produced for a project.

Other factors

This chapter has focused on the financial analysis of a project. It is wise to consider non-financial aspects such as commercial, production, safety, environmental and technical risk. These can be quantified, and using the technique known as the Balanced Scorecard a weighted score for a project can be calculated – see Chapter 8.

13

Where is all our cash? Managing working capital

When business improvements are sought, we are often asked to manage our working capital more closely. This is because of all the monies tied up in a company, it is only the working capital that can be managed on a day-to-day basis. The fixed assets such as land, plant and machinery can be revalued on a one-off basis but this cannot be done every time we are looking to improve business performance!

Also, while revaluing assets may produce a paper profit or loss, it does nothing to generate cash unless we sell part or all of these items. Managing working capital on the other hand can generate or consume cash.

You will recall from earlier chapters that working capital is made up of three main elements – stocks, debtors and creditors – and these will be considered in turn. Clearly, a service-based organisation has minimal stocks, and so the focus must be on debtors and creditors.

Stock (inventories)

Stock is generally made up of three elements which we will now consider in turn:

Raw materials

Raw materials are goods that have been delivered to our company's warehouse but have not yet been taken into the production area for conversion. As these are part of working capital, it would seem that minimising raw material stock is ideal. However, this must be offset by the economic order quantities available from suppliers.

Another approach is just in time (JIT) deliveries of raw materials. In this way, goods can be delivered directly to the production area, eliminating any raw material store. The aim is to get our supplier to carry the stock rather than doing this ourselves.

Work in progress (WIP)

WIP involves any product once it has left the raw material store until it is declared available for sale and delivery to customers. In a multi-step process this can also involve intermediate products awaiting conversion to the next stage. To reduce working capital we must consider reducing these buffer stocks, eliminating or combining stages in the production process, reducing the overall production cycle time, and minimising raw material and finished goods stocks in the production area.

The amount of WIP can also be badly affected when different stages of the manufacturing process takes place on different sites. This is common when companies acquire an 'upstream' or 'downstream' processor. In these cases the stock travelling between sites must also be taken into account.

Finally, we must examine how long it takes for products to be cleared for sale by our quality control (QC) procedures. Some organisations have huge stocks sitting in a pending bay awaiting clearance from QC.

Finished goods

'Finished goods' refers to the stock sitting in the warehouse awaiting sale and delivery to our customers. Some of this may have been in the warehouse for a long time, and if the goods have a shelf-life they may be unsaleable. In these circumstances we must consult our technical staff to find out what options we have to dispose of slow-moving items. Should we repack or reprocess the stock, sell it at a discount or dispose of it altogether? Good sales and operations planning can reduce or eliminate the need for finished goods stocks.

Examples of best practice in stock management are the car manufacturers. They use JIT to have components delivered directly to their production lines at the exact point where the component is fitted to the car. Then they ask their suppliers not to invoice them until a short time later when the finished car rolls off the end of the production line. In this way they minimise or eliminate both raw material stock and work in progress, as all their stock is now in finished goods.

Debtors

'Debtors' refers to the amount of money owed to us by our customers. This is directly related to how long customers take to pay their bills. The longer we give them to pay, the more we will have owed to us at any one time. Inevitably customers are late in paying their bills. Timely monitoring and enforcement of the terms under which you do business can help you manage your debtors better. Other factors can include invoice accuracy, correct addressing of invoicing to the appropriate department/location at your customer, offering a prompt payment discount (a small percentage discount can have a disproportionate effect on payment times), and establishing maximum credit limits after which further orders cannot be accepted.

Improvements can be brought about by more regular invoicing of your customers. Imagine if you only invoice once a month. The value of a whole month's worth of deliveries could be building up before you even invoice the customer. With today's electronic payment systems it is often possible to increase invoicing frequency with no additional workload after the initial set-up.

In all these areas the key is communicating the issues to your customers and negotiating better terms rather than simply imposing them.

How long does it take you to invoice your customers?

A private hospital with a turnover of £36 million per year was taking 15 days to collect all the information on what services and drugs patients had used in the various departments before sending out bills. With sales of £100,000 per day this was equivalent to £1.5 million that they had not yet invoiced.

Halving this delay in issuing their bills would release £750,000 of cash, which could then be used to pay off loans, buy new equipment etc – a sum definitely worth working towards.

Creditors

Creditors provide a mechanism for funding your business. The more credit we can get from our suppliers (ie the longer we take to pay our bills), the better our cash flow position. Once again the key to success is to negotiate better terms and then not pay these bills until the day they are due.

Asking your suppliers to invoice you monthly or quarterly rather than every time they deliver can improve your working capital. This is because the amount outstanding builds up before you are billed, and therefore you end up with more credit from your supplier.

It is possible to have negative working capital when you can get more credit from your suppliers than you give your customers. Consider a trading company that buys from an overseas supplier with three-month terms (ie 90 days to pay the supplier's bill) and sells to its customers on 30 days. This business can receive the cash on two out of the three months' worth of bought-in stock before having to pay its supplier anything.

Supermarkets also work on this basis, effectively selling to consumers for cash and paying suppliers after 30–60 days. This is why many retailers have started offering financial services. They generate a lot of cash, which they can then use before having to pay their suppliers.

Why payment terms matter

Getting extended credit terms from suppliers is worth more than any non-financially aware business person ever imagines – purchasers take note.

Giving extended credit to customers is more expensive than any non-financially aware business person ever imagines – salespeople take note.

Write-offs

In all the above examples, where items are carried in the books which will never realistically be realised (ie turned into cash) then we must consider writing down their book value, or writing them off completely.

If we consider reducing the value of something on the top half of the balance sheet, then we must reduce the value of the bottom half of the balance sheet, otherwise the books will no longer balance. This is done by showing a loss for the same amount as the value we are writing off. In other words, it becomes a write-off cost, which reduces the number carried across from the P&L account into the bottom half of the balance sheet as retained earnings.

Similarly, revaluing an asset by increasing its book value will result in a paper profit to balance the bottom half of the books. This will appear as an additional line in the P&L account.

Both these items can sometimes appear in the accounts under various terms (eg stock adjustments) and can be found at any level between the top and bottom line of the P&L account.

Cash flow implications of working capital

As we have already seen, when considering the cash tied up in a business, there are two main areas: fixed assets and working capital. Because we cannot do much to affect the day-to-day value of our fixed assets, managers concentrate all their efforts on managing working capital! Table 13.1 gives a summary of impact of each element of working capital.

Table 13.1 Impact of different elements of working capital

Item of working capital	Cash implications
Stock (inventories)	**Decrease** in stocks **releases** cash
	Increase in stocks **consumes** cash
Debtors (receivables)	**Decrease** in total value of debtors **releases** cash
– money owed by customers	**Increase** in total value of debtors **consumes** cash
Creditors (payables)	**Increase** in total value of creditors **releases** cash
– credit from suppliers	**Decrease** in total value of creditors **reduces** cash available

Generally, managing working capital means reducing working capital to release cash. This means reducing stocks, and money owed by customers, and increasing the credit from suppliers.

Working capital will also change as our volume of business changes. Suppose we are a company with monthly sales of £100,000 and it takes two months to get our bills paid. This means at any time we will have two months' worth of sales, or £200,000, owed to us. Now we are really successful and grow our sales to £150,000 per month. How much will we now have owed to us – £300,000! Where does the money come from, then, to fund this £100,000 increase in working capital? Well, it must come from somewhere. Perhaps there is enough cash in the business, or perhaps we can get another loan. This is one of the reasons that companies get into cash flow difficulties when they expand too fast.

Lastly, consider what happens when closing down a business, perhaps because cash flow problems just got too much. Inevitably there will be monies owed from customers yet to be paid. In the months following the winding up of that company, cash will start flowing in as these invoices get paid. It is at times like these that you might start to regret closing the business: you are cash rich for the first time in your life! It is an irony of business that cash flow can be at its best when you are selling the least...

Glossary of financial terms

absorption costing Full costing. Calculated by dividing the total fixed costs incurred during a period by the units sold. The allocated fixed cost is added to the variable cost to give the full cost of the product.

accounting The process of measuring and summarising financial information about the activities of a business to provide information to shareholders, managers and employees about what is happening in the business. *See* management accounting, financial accounting.

accounting conventions Principles used by accountants when preparing accounts so that there is a degree of comparability between the accounts of different companies, and between accounts for the same company in different periods. If any changes are made in the way that accounting conventions have been applied, these must be disclosed by the auditors in the notes to the annual accounts.

accounts (UK) Financial Statements (US) Books. The records kept by a business of its financial activities.

accounts payable (US)   Creditors (UK). Money owing to suppliers for goods and services purchased but not yet paid for.

accounts receivable (US)   Debtors (UK). Money owing from customers for goods or services supplied and invoiced, but not yet paid for. *See also* DSO.

accrual accounting   This recognises the occurrence of income and expense irrespective of whether cash has moved in or out of the company at the time the transaction occurs. For example, when a piece of equipment is bought, the expense will be recorded, even though payment for it may only be made several months later. If accrual accounting is not used, the system is called 'receipts and payments' or 'cash accounting'.

accumulated depreciation   This shows the amount of depreciation suffered to date. When subtracted from the cost of the assets, the result is the net book value.

acid test (US)   *See* quick ratio (UK).

activity ratio   Asset turnover, spin. Sales revenues divided by net (or total) assets. This shows the efficiency with which the assets used by the business are being used to generate sales, regardless of the source of the capital. Retailing and service industries typically have high activity ratios. Manufacturing industries are typically capital-intensive, with high fixed and current asset figures, and low activity ratios.

allocation of costs   Giving the costs to the product or division that 'owns' them, eg accounting the cost of an advertising campaign against income from the product advertised.

amortisation   Periodically recorded expenses which show the gradual reduction of value of an asset or an obligation. Usually refers to goodwill, patents and other intangible assets, or issuing expenses of debt securities.

assets   The things owned by the business. These may include fixed assets, current assets and intangible assets.

asset turnover   ATO; *see* activity ratio.

auditing   The process of checking the books and accounting systems of a company to verify that the company's accounts give a true and fair view of its financial situation.

auditors' report   A limited company must by law produce a set of accounts every year, and the auditors must report on whether the accounts provide a true and fair statement of the company's business. The auditors have to investigate the accounts to establish this, and if they are not satisfied with them they produce a 'qualified report' in which they say what they consider to be wrong or uncertain in the accounts. A qualified report from the auditors can be damaging to the public image of a company and its share price.

authorised capital   The amount of share capital that the company has been authorised to issue. Stamp duty is paid at the time of authorisation, and if the directors wish to issue further shares once the authorised capital is fully issued, they must get approval from the shareholders. Once authorised, shares may be issued at the discretion of the company's board of directors.

bad debts   Accounts receivable (US) or debtors (UK) that will never be collected. 'Writing off' a bad debt means reducing the debtors figure by the amount written off, and putting that in the P&L account as an expense against profits.

balance sheet   A snapshot of the financial position of the business at a given time. It summarises all the assets owned by the business, the equity invested, and all the liabilities; in lay terms, what the business has, and where it came from.

bonds   Debentures. A way of borrowing.

book value   Net book value. The difference between the purchase cost of an asset and its accumulated depreciation.

break-even point   The volume of sales at which total sales equals total costs, and the company makes neither profit nor loss. At this point the contribution exactly equals the fixed costs. Break-even volume (in unit sales) is calculated by dividing total fixed costs by the unit contribution. Break-even sales turnover is calculated by multiplying the break-even volume by the unit selling price.

budget (UK)   Business plan (US), a management plan for financial achievement over a specified period. This needs to be supported by an action plan that will give rise to the required financial results. The budget provides a way of coordinating the activities of different departments within a company, and for testing the viability of planned activities. The amount of commitment shown by employees to a budget is proportional to their involvement in creating the budget, and the amount of personal benefit they expect to receive from achieving it.

budgetary control   This is a process of setting budgets, measuring actual results, and comparing the actual against the budget to see where variances occur, and what new plans must be made.

burden (US)   Overhead costs, indirect expenses. *See also* overheads.

capital   Used in several different senses (eg savings, cash reserves, equity in a business), it usually means money. Capital investment means the purchase of long-term assets such as machines, as opposed to goods for resale, services etc.

capital employed   The money used to finance a business. Calculated as share capital plus reserves (qv), plus long-term loans; or as total assets less current liabilities.

capital expenditure   The purchase of fixed assets.

capital surplus   Money received from the sale of shares, over and above their face value. For example, if 100 new £1 shares are sold at the current market value of £5 each, £100 will be added to the share capital account of the business, and £400 will be recorded as capital surplus. The capital surplus indicates the company's ability to raise further money through selling shares, and is thus a measure of financial strength.

cash   Literally money, or money in bank accounts that can be withdrawn at short notice.

cash flow   The difference between the cash received (from sales etc) and the cash paid out for costs and expenses.
    Used loosely, this term may refer either to trading cash flow or net cash flow.
    Trading cash flow is calculated as the profit after tax (net income (US)), plus depreciation. This shows how much cash the business generated that could be used to fund its expansion or other activities.
    But for various reasons, including the use of accrual accounting, this will only give an indication of the actual cash flow that occurred. The company's net cash flow is the net result of its trading cash flow (its profit adjusted for non-cash income or expenses), net asset cash flow (the increase or decrease in net assets) and financial cash flow (the net in- or out-flow of funds due to changes in share capital, borrowings, and dividends). *See* funds flow.

cash flow forecast   A projection of the expected movements of cash in and out of the company over a given period. This has no direct relationship to profitability.

cash flow statement   Statement of sources and applications of funds (UK), statement of changes in financial position (US). An analysis of cash flows from operations, working capital and fixed asset movements over a period.

chairman's statement   A statement made by the company's chairman about its activities during the past accounting period, and its plans and prospects for the future. Part of the annual report.

common stock (US)   Ordinary shares (UK). The amount paid in by shareholders for shares at par value.

consistency convention   An accounting convention which requires that accounting entries be treated in the same way in each set of accounts, so that meaningful comparisons can be made between them. If a change in accounting methods is made, it must be reported in the notes to the accounts, and in some cases two sets of accounts are presented to show what the results would have looked like without the change in accounting methods.

consolidation   The creation of one set of accounts summarising the activity of a parent company and all its subsidiaries. The consolidated accounts may look quite different from the accounts of individual companies in the group, because profits in one area and losses in another may be offset, and costs reallocated between lines in the P&L account.

contingent liabilities   These are liabilities that the company may incur, or will probably incur, soon after the date of the balance sheet. They must be listed in notes to the accounts when annual accounts are published. An example would be a lawsuit in process against the company, which if lost would cause the company to suffer significant costs.

contribution   Sales revenue less variable costs. This amount is a contribution to cover the total fixed costs of the company, and surplus would become a profit. Also sometimes called gross profit, gross margin or standard margin.

cost–benefit analysis   The incremental benefits less the incremental costs of any change in investment or operations.

cost of ownership   The cost of acquiring and operating an asset.

cost of sales   The directly attributable costs of providing a product or service. In retailing, generally the purchase price of the goods, sometimes plus the cost of carriage in and/or out. In manufacturing, the cost of raw materials plus variable labour cost, sometimes plus depreciation on manufacturing equipment.

creative accounting   Many aspects of accounting depend on judgement rather than objective fact, and therefore accounts for the same business could be drawn up to look quite different, depending on the judgements used. There is room for considerable creativity in this process, which at best results in a more accurate reflection of the business's health, and at worst amounts to fraud.

creditors (UK)   Accounts payable (US). The amount owing to suppliers for goods and services received but not yet paid for.

creditors' days (UK)   Payables' days (US). Days' credit taken. Trade creditors divided by average daily purchases, or creditors × 365/cost of sales. This shows the average time taken by the business to pay its suppliers. The longer it takes, the more it is using suppliers' money to finance its own operations. Financially this is a good thing, but taking too much credit may upset suppliers and endanger future supplies.

current assets   Assets that are consumed or sold as the main business of the company, such as cash, debtors, stocks of raw material, work in progress, and finished goods, and prepayments the company has made for goods or services.

current liabilities   All debts due for repayment within one year. These include trade creditors, overdrafts or short-term loans, and any long-term loans coming due for repayment.

current ratio   Current assets divided by current liabilities. An indication of liquidity, or the company's ability to raise money quickly to repay short-term liabilities. In many businesses, over 2:1.

days' credit taken   *See* creditors' days (UK), payables' days (US).

days' sales outstanding (DSO)   *See* debtors' days (UK), receivables' days (US).

debentures   Bonds. A way of borrowing money; usually organised through a bank, but the lender receives a note stating how much interest will be paid, and when, as well as the amount and repayment date for the loan. This note is negotiable, and both interest and capital are repaid to the bearer on due dates, not usually to the original lender.

debt/equity ratio   A measure of gearing (UK) or leverage (US). The ratio of a company's borrowings to its share capital plus reserves. Calculated in two ways, either as total liabilities divided by shareholders' equity, or as long-term liabilities/shareholders' equity.

debtors (UK)   Accounts receivable (US). The money owed to a company by its customers for goods or services supplied and invoiced, but not yet paid for.

debtors' days   A measure of the average time taken for credit customers to pay for their purchases. Debtors divided by average daily rate of sales.

deferred taxes   Taxes that have already been charged against profits in the P&L account, but have not yet been paid. They show on the balance sheet as a current liability.

depreciation   Fixed assets have a useful life of several years. When they are bought, the value of the asset is capitalised, or written on to the balance sheet. It is not treated as an expense of the business, to be recorded on the P&L account as a charge against profits.

Depreciation is a way of charging the cost of using the asset (which will eventually have to be replaced) against the periods during which it is used. A portion of the cost is deducted from the balance sheet value (book value) each year, and put in the P&L account as an expense. No cash transaction occurs. At the end of the asset's expected life it is 'written off', or listed as having no value in the balance sheet, though it may still be working well, and may have market value.

dividends   Payments from profits to the shareholders. Dividends paid out will be shown on the bottom of the P&L account, dividends proposed but not yet paid will be among the current liabilities on the balance sheet.

DSO   *See* days' sales outstanding.

earnings per share (EPS)   Net profit divided by the number of ordinary shares issued. A measure of the efficiency with which shareholders' funds are being used to generate profit, which can then be used either to expand the business and increase the value of the assets, or to pay dividends.

EBIT (US)   Earnings before interest and tax. *See* operating profit.

EBITDA   Earnings before interest, tax, depreciation and amortisation.

economic profit   The concept of adjusting profit to take account of the opportunity cost of the money invested in the business. This is calculated by subtracting a capital charge (the net asset value of a business multiplied by the weighted average cost of capital – WACC rate) from the profit generated.

EPS   *See* Earnings per Share.

equity   The net worth, or balance sheet value, of the business to its owners. If all the assets were sold off at their present book value, and all loans and other debts repaid, the remainder would be the shareholders' equity. Calculated by adding share capital, capital surplus and reserves.

extraordinary items   Events with a significant effect on the company's financial results, which are of a unique or non-recurring nature, separate from the normal trading activities of the business. Examples include purchase or sale of a subsidiary business, changes in accounting procedures, profit or loss caused by major devaluation of a foreign currency etc.

fair market value   The price a willing buyer would pay to a willing seller if neither was under any compulsion to make the deal.

FASB (US)   Financial Accounting Standards Board, which lays down the rules for accounting practices in the United States.

FIFO   First In First Out. A method of valuing inventories. *See also* LIFO.

financial accounting   The preparation of annual reports and other items for external interested parties, and to satisfy the legal requirements of government.

financial cash flow   The net cash flow resulting from changes in loans, share capital and the payment of dividends.

financial statements (US)   Accounts (UK). Reports on the activities and financial position of a business, including the balance sheet, P&L account, statement of changes in financial position (US) or funds flow statement (UK) and notes to the accounts.

fixed assets   Things owned by the company, not intended for resale, and used to carry on its business. Buildings and machines are usually fixed assets, though not to the companies that make them.

fixed costs   Overheads. Costs that do not vary in proportion to the volume of sales within the range of activities and the timescale being considered. Examples include advertising, administration and telephone bills. They include most costs other than cost of sales, tax and dividends.

full costing   Calculating the cost of each unit of sales, including direct costs (labour, materials) and indirect costs or overheads. Calculated by dividing the total costs and expenses for the period by the number of units sold. This can cause confusion because it varies with the volume of sales, but it gives a realistic estimate of cost for pricing decisions.

funds flow   The changes in the value of balance sheet items from one period to the next either absorb or release funds. If the net changes in fixed assets and working capital release funds, the company will be able to pay off liabilities such as bank loans; if the net changes absorb funds, this requires increased borrowing or an increase in share capital.

funds flow statement (UK)   Statement of sources and applications of funds (UK), cash flow statement, statement of changes in financial position (US). A summary of funds flows in a period.

GAAP (US)   Generally accepted accounting principles. Equivalent to SSAPs (UK). The detailed set of conventions and practices that guide the preparation of financial accounts.

gearing (UK)   Leverage (US). A measure of the extent to which borrowed funds have been used to increase the power of the shareholders' equity to earn profits. High leverage is desirable in low-risk businesses because the extra profit is paid to the existing shareholders. In risky businesses, or in times of high or unstable interest rates, low leverage is preferable. Defined in various ways, such as total assets divided by shareholders' equity.

It is only worth borrowing to expand a business if the internal return on investment (ORA or RONA) is expected to be significantly higher than the interest rates payable on new borrowings.

going concern convention   The accounting convention which requires that unless stated otherwise, accounts are drawn on the basis that the business will continue to operate indefinitely.

goodwill   When a business is sold, the price paid is usually greater than the total asset value as shown on the balance sheet. The difference, which represents the buyer's expectation that it will generate profits in future, is called goodwill, and is put among the fixed assets of the buying company's balance sheet. Goodwill is usually depreciated over the first few years after the purchase.

gross margin   Gross profit. Sales less cost of sales, less factory overheads in a manufacturing business. GPM or manufacturing margin.

gross profit   *See* gross margin.

historical cost   The actual cost of buying an asset at the time it was purchased. Normal accounting values all assets at historical cost (less accumulated depreciation) rather than at their current or replacement cost. In times of high inflation, current cost accounting may be used, but this has certain anomalies since usually fixed assets are valued at current cost, and inventories at historical cost, and the sum is not fully meaningful.

income statement (US)   Profit & Loss account (UK). A summary of the income and expenses of a business during an accounting period, eg a year.

incremental cost   The extra cost associated with an action, eg hiring a staff member or producing another unit.

intangible assets   Non-physical assets of the company, such as patents, trademarks, goodwill and know-how.

interest cover   Operating profit divided by interest payable. A measure of safety, the ability of the business to service its loans.

internal rate of return (IRR)   The discount rate at which the net present value of a project is zero. Found by trial and error. Because of the nature of mathematics, some projects have two different IRRs, each of which gives zero net present value.

investments   Money invested in other companies, deposited in the bank, or otherwise used to generate income of a non-trading nature.

IRR   *See* Internal Rate of Return.

junk bonds   Bonds issued by companies with a very small asset base, consequently offering a high-risk investment, typically with high interest.

leverage (US)   *See* gearing (UK).

liabilities   The value of goods, services and loans provided to the business (not by shareholders) which it must repay one day. Those due for repayment within 12 months are current or short term; all others are long term. *See also* short-term liabilities, long-term liabilities.
    Traditionally, shareholders' funds have been seen as liabilities of the business, because if the business was liquidated it would owe them back to the shareholders. But when people talk of the liabilities of the business, they usually mean the other liabilities, as described above.

LIFO   Last In First Out. A method of costing inventory. *See also* FIFO.

liquidity   The ability of a business to pay the costs and expenses that it needs to pay in the near future. A crude measure is the quick ratio or acid test. Balance sheet measures of liquidity do not indicate the full extent of the company's short-term cash requirements, because items like salaries not yet incurred, and materials ordered but not yet received, may add significantly to the short-term cash requirements shown in the books.

long-term liabilities   Long-term debt. Loans and other debts of the business that are not due for payment within the next year.

loss   When the costs and expenses during a period are greater than the sales revenue, the business makes a loss, and the shareholders' equity is reduced by the amount of the loss.

management accounting   The production of financial information for internal use, to support management decision making. Management accounts include budgets, cash flow forecasts, product-by-product cost analyses and so forth. The emphasis in management accounting is on having useful information at the right time. This is different from financial accounting, where the emphasis is on accuracy and fitting legally defined ways of presenting the information.

marginal costing   Determining the cost of selling one additional item, usually direct labour and materials, plus any variable overheads such as sales commission. Marginal costing is useful in setting prices for special deals such as a non-recurring export order, but full costing (qv) should be used for most purposes, as it gives a truer picture of costs.

marketable securities   Bonds, bills and shares in other companies that can be sold readily on stock or financial markets. Treated as part of current assets and working capital if they are to be sold within one year; as fixed assets if kept as an investment.

market leader   The company with greatest sales in a given market is the leader. In some markets the leader's share is very high, but in most markets the leader has no more than 15–20 per cent of the market. Leadership usually carries a strong strategic advantage. The leader can price 7–12 per cent higher than the next competitor for a product of the same quality; its advertising is more effective because the product or brand name is more readily recognised by customers; and the profitability that comes from large sales and high prices enables it to stay at the front of product development and service.

market value   The amount for which an asset can be sold.

matching convention   An accounting convention that requires the cost of producing goods or services to be shown in accounts in the period when they are sold, so that profit for each period can be calculated. *See* timing convention, accrual accounting

materiality convention   An accounting convention that allows non-standard accounting practices to be used if their effects are so small as to be insignificant in the context of the whole business. For a multinational, amounts of millions are sometimes not material!

money measurement convention   An accounting convention from which accounts record only events and items that can be described in money value terms. 'Our people are our greatest asset' is nonsense in accounting terms, because people cannot be valued and included on the balance sheet.

net asset cash flow   The net cash used or generated by increases and decreases in assets and non-interest-bearing liabilities.

net assets   Total assets less all non-interest-bearing debts. The total investment in the business financed by shareholders' equity and interest-bearing debt.

net assets per share   Net assets divided by the number of shares issued.

net book value   The value of fixed assets less accumulated depreciation.

net current assets   Net working capital. Current assets less current liabilities.

net income (US)   *See* net profit (UK).

net present value   The sum of present values of all the cash flows projected over the life of a project.

net profit (UK)   Net income (US). The profit after interest and tax, available for dividends or retention in the business. Note that the existence of profit does not guarantee the availability of cash.

net realisable value   The value that would become cash if the asset were sold.

net working capital   Current assets less current liabilities. The more interest-free credit a company gets from suppliers, tax authorities etc, the less money it needs to provide (from shareholders or loans) to finance its working capital needs. In a few kinds of business, cash from sales is received before purchases and expenses have to be paid, and working capital may be negative. This can happen in supermarkets and airlines, and provides a fund of customer-financed money.

net worth   The net book value of the shareholders' equity; total assets less all liabilities.

NPV   *See* Net Present Value.

operating profit   PBIT (UK), EBIT (US), also given many company-specific names, eg MAUI (AT&T), net contribution

(Abbott), TP (Unilever). Sales revenue less cost of sales, selling and operating expenses. The amount of money available to cover interest expenses, taxes, and provide a return to the investors. This is the level of profit managed by most managers, who do not control the financing of their operations and therefore whose results should be measured before interest.

operating return on assets   ORA, RONA. The internal return on investment of the business; operating profit divided by (net) assets.

opportunity cost   The notional cost (loss of earnings) that results from not making alternative use of resources. For example, with idle factory space, one opportunity cost of an expansion of machinery into the space is the rental income that would be earned if the space were rented to a third party. Another might be the interest that could be earned on the money invested in machinery, if instead it was deposited in the bank.

ORA   (Operating Return on Assets), *see* return on net assets.

other income   Income from subsidiary companies, investments, royalties etc that do not form part of the principal trading activity of the company.

overheads (UK)   Burden (US). Expenses of the business that do not contribute directly to the value of the product or service provided. Generally, fixed costs.

owners' equity   Net worth. The total of share capital and reserves. The total funds invested by shareholders for the purchase of shares, and profits reinvested by the company. Total assets less total liabilities.

P&L   *See* Profit and Loss account.

payables (US)   *See* creditors (UK).

payables' days (US)   *See* creditors' days (UK).

payback period   The time needed for cash inflows for a project to exceed the cash outflows incurred at the start, so that net cash flow to date becomes positive. If the present values of future cash flows are calculated, payback may take far longer than on the crude figures.

PBIT   Profit before Interest and Tax. *See* operating profit.

P/E ratio   *See* price/earnings ratio.

prepayments   Goods or services that the company has paid for but not yet received; these are a current asset.

present value   The value in today's terms of a cash flow at a future time, discounted at an appropriate rate to reflect the alternative use to which funds could be put now. *See* time value of money.

price/earnings ratio   The market price of a share, divided by the earnings per share. A measure of how long, at the current rate of earnings, a shareholder has to wait for his earnings (whether paid out as dividends or retained) to total the current price of the share. A kind of rough payback per share bought today.

prime cost   The direct cost of labour and materials used to produce the product or deliver the service.

profit   The increase in value of a business over a period. When used without qualification, it may refer to contribution, gross profit, operating profit, earnings (US) or profit (UK) before tax, or even net income (US) or net profit (UK). Profit occurs when sales revenue exceeds costs and expenses. It has no automatic short-term connection with cash flow.

profitability   Operating profit divided by sales revenue × 100. Also sometimes used to refer to return on investment, ROI.

Profit and Loss (P&L) account (UK)   Income statement (US). A summary of the income and expenses of a business during an accounting period, usually a year.

prospectus   A document put out by a company wishing to raise finance through the sale of shares. Typically it will give the company's recent history, and explain why it needs the extra funds and how they will represent a sound investment.

provisions   When goods or services have been received by a company, but have not yet been invoiced, the expense is shown as a provision. Provisions may also be made for uncertain events such as the occurrence of bad debts, and taxes not yet assessed. They depend on the accrual accounting concept.

prudence convention   An accounting convention which requires that all possible costs are taken into account, but sales are only accounted for when invoiced.

qualified report   *See* auditors' report.

quick ratio (UK)   Acid test (US). Liquid assets (cash + receivables/ debtors) divided by current liabilities (payables/creditors + loans due inside one year). A crude measure of liquidity.

ratio analysis   Ratios between balance sheet items or P&L account items often provide an insight into the level of risk in a company, its effectiveness at generating profit for the shareholders, and so forth. The simple calculation of these ratios, usually by dividing one number by another, and their interpretation, is ratio analysis.

receivables' days   A measure of the average time taken for credit customers to pay for their purchases. Accounts receivable divided by the average daily rate of sales.

relevant range   The range of values over which cost analysis is valid because costs behave uniformly, in drawing break-even graphs.

replacement value   The cost of replacing an asset with a similar new one.

reserves   *See* retained earnings.

retained earnings   Reserves, retentions, ploughbacks. The amount of past profits that have not been paid out as taxes or dividends, but kept in the business to increase the shareholders' equity.

return on assets (ROA)   ROTA, ROGA. Net profit (UK) or net income (US) divided by total assets (= fixed assets + current assets).

return on capital employed   ROCE.

return on equity (ROE)   Net income/net profit divided by total shareholders' equity. A measure of the effectiveness of the business in utilising shareholders' funds to generate wealth. It does not tell you how much of the profit was paid out in dividends, and how much was retained as reserves.

return on investment (ROI)   A measure of the ability of the business to use the money invested in it to generate profits. A loosely defined phrase, which may be used to refer to almost any return ratio, and sometimes referred to as profitability.

return on net assets (RONA) (UK)   ORA (US). Operating profit divided by net assets. The key measure of operating management performance. It removes the effects of financing decisions and tax (not usually controlled by the operating manager) and shows the ability of the business to cover interest charges and use loan financing. It also shows the inherent profitability of the business. *See also* operating return on assets.

return on sales (ROS)   Profit or earnings as a percentage of sales. This examines performance in relation to the bottom line (profit or earnings).

return on shareholders' funds (ROSF)   Return on equity (ROE).

ROA   *See* Return on Assets.

ROCE   Return on Capital Employed.

ROE   *See* Return on Equity, return on shareholders' funds.

ROGA   (Return on Gross Assets), *see* return on assets.

RONA   *See* Return on Net Assets.

ROS   *See* Return on Sales.

ROSF   *See* Return on Shareholders' Funds.

ROTA   (Return on Total Assets), *see* return on assets.

sensitivity analysis   Analysis of a new project or an existing business to see the relative sensitivity of profits and cash flows to changes in various factors such as sales volume, interest rates, labour costs etc.

share capital   The money invested in the business by shareholders.

shareholders (UK)   Shareowners (US). The owners of the business, who receive a return on their investment through dividends paid to them, or through the growth in market value of their shares. They risk not receiving dividends, and losing some or all the value of their investment, if the company performs badly.

shareholders' wealth   The market value of the company's shares. Values rise when the company reports good, steady and growing profits; when results are consistently in line with the company's own predictions; and when present or potential shareholders expect them to rise. They fall for the converse reasons. The market price of shares has no direct link to the asset value of the company as shown by its balance sheet.

share price   The price of the company's shares on the stock markets.

share surplus   Money paid by shareholders when buying newly issued shares, in excess of the face or 'par' value of the share.

short-term liabilities   Amounts that the business must pay within one year, shown on the balance sheet. They do not give a true indication of the financial commitments of the business, because such things as lease agreements, salary bills and supply contracts may require substantial resources in the near future, but do not show in the balance sheet as liabilities until the services are received. *See also* liabilities.

standard costing   The process of allocating a nominal cost to goods or services to allow pricing and other decisions to be made. When the actual costs incurred are higher or lower than the standard, the difference is shown on the P&L account as under- or over-recoveries.

stock   Stocks of raw materials, work in progress, finished goods and spare parts.

strategic planning   Planning related to the long-term goals and performance of the business. Frequently begins with SWOT analysis.

subsidiary company   A company, 50 per cent or more of whose shares are owned by the holding company.

SWOT analysis The detailed consideration of the internal Strengths and Weaknesses of the business, and the Opportunities and Threats it faces from the outside. Internal scanning is often done by function, eg research and development, finance, operations, marketing, sales etc. Outside scanning may look at technology, markets and demographics, competitors, legal changes, politics locally and in other countries, and so on.

tangible assets Physical possessions of the business. *See also* intangible assets.

time value of money The concept that money in the hand today is worth more than the same amount received in the future, because it could be put to work earning compound interest for the period between. Even without inflation, the present value is higher than the future value if there are opportunities to invest.

timing convention An accounting convention that recognises only those events within a set period as being relevant to the accounts for that period. *See* accrual accounting, matching convention.

total assets All the valuable possessions of the business. Includes tangible and intangible assets, both current and fixed.

trading cash flow The cash flow resulting directly from the company's trading activity. Net profit adjusted for any non-cash expenses or incomes, eg depreciation.

unit cost The total cost of an output divided by the number of units. Units may be physical, eg cars, or not, eg covers in a restaurant, bed-nights, passenger-miles.

value added Sales revenue less all bought-in goods and services.

variable costs   Costs which change in direct proportion to sales revenue, over their relevant range (qv). Example: cost of goods sold in a retail business.

weighted average cost of capital (WACC)   The percentage charge levied for money tied up in a company. *See also* economic profit.

working capital   The value of assets used (consumed) in the main trading activities of the company, eg cash, raw materials, work in progress, credit given to customers. In many businesses the investment in working capital is considerably greater than that needed in fixed assets.

zero-based budgeting   A system of budgeting in which historical spending patterns are explicitly ignored, and each budget item is justified *de novo* at the level proposed for the coming period.

With over 42 years of publishing, more than 80 million people have succeeded in business with thanks to **Kogan Page**

www.koganpage.com